First World War
and Army of Occupation
War Diary
France, Belgium and Germany

57 DIVISION
172 Infantry Brigade
King's (Liverpool Regiment)
2/10 Battalion
30 January 1917 - 4 July 1918

WO95/2985/6

The Naval & Military Press Ltd
www.nmarchive.com
Published in association with The National Archives

Published by

The Naval & Military Press Ltd

Unit 10 Ridgewood Industrial Park,

Uckfield, East Sussex,

TN22 5QE England

Tel: +44 (0) 1825 749494

www.naval-military-press.com

www.nmarchive.com

This diary has been reprinted in facsimile from the original. Any imperfections are inevitably reproduced and the quality may fall short of modern type and cartographic standards.

© Crown Copyright
Images reproduced by permission of The National Archives, London, England, 2015.

Contents

Document type	Place/Title	Date From	Date To
Heading	WO95/2985/6 57 Divn. 172 Inf. Brig 2/10 King's Liverpool Regt 1917 Feb-1918 July		
War Diary	Blackdown Barracks	30/01/1917	01/02/1917
War Diary	Folkestune Boulogne	02/02/1917	03/02/1917
War Diary	Hazebrouck	04/02/1917	04/02/1917
War Diary	Bois Grenier Trenches	04/02/1917	11/02/1917
War Diary	Erquinghem	11/02/1917	15/02/1917
War Diary	Bois Grenier Trenches	15/02/1917	17/02/1917
War Diary	Trenches Bois Grenier	18/02/1917	20/02/1917
War Diary	Erquinghem	21/02/1917	23/02/1917
War Diary	Trenchs Bois Grenier	27/02/1917	27/02/1917
War Diary	Blackdown Barracks	16/02/1917	16/02/1917
War Diary	Southampton	16/02/1917	16/02/1917
War Diary	Havre	17/02/1917	18/02/1917
War Diary	Blackdown Barracks	18/02/1917	18/02/1917
War Diary	Southampton	18/02/1917	18/02/1917
War Diary	Bailleul	19/02/1917	19/02/1917
War Diary	Southampton	19/02/1917	19/02/1917
War Diary	Blackdown Barracks	16/02/1917	16/02/1917
War Diary	Southampton	16/02/1917	16/02/1917
War Diary	Havre	17/02/1917	18/02/1917
War Diary	Blackdown Barracks	18/02/1917	18/02/1917
War Diary	Southampton	18/02/1917	18/02/1917
War Diary	Bailleul	19/02/1917	19/02/1917
War Diary	Southampton	19/02/1917	19/02/1917
War Diary	Sec Bois	20/02/1917	20/02/1917
War Diary	Southampton	20/02/1917	20/02/1917
War Diary	Sec Bois	21/02/1917	21/02/1917
War Diary	Southampton	21/02/1917	21/02/1917
War Diary	Sec Bois	20/02/1917	20/02/1917
War Diary	Southampton	20/02/1917	20/02/1917
War Diary	Sec-Bois	21/02/1917	21/02/1917
War Diary	Southampton	21/02/1917	21/02/1917
War Diary	Sec Bois	22/02/1917	22/02/1917
War Diary	Havre	22/02/1917	22/02/1917
War Diary	Sec Bois	23/02/1917	23/02/1917
War Diary	Bailleul	23/02/1917	23/02/1917
War Diary	Estaires	23/02/1917	24/02/1917
War Diary	Sec Bois	22/02/1917	22/02/1917
War Diary	Havre	22/02/1917	22/02/1917
War Diary	Sec Bois	23/02/1917	23/02/1917
War Diary	Bailleut	23/02/1917	23/02/1917
War Diary	Estaires	23/02/1917	24/02/1917
War Diary	Estaires Trenchs Bois Grenier (Ref Trench Map Bois Grenier 36 N W 4 Edition 6.d. Scale 1.10000	26/02/1917	28/02/1917
War Diary	Trenchs Bois Grenier	01/03/1917	06/03/1917
War Diary	Erquinghem	07/03/1917	09/03/1917
War Diary	La Rolanderie Rue Marle	10/03/1917	12/03/1917
War Diary	Trenches (Bois Grenier Sector)	13/03/1917	21/03/1917
War Diary	La Rolanderie Billets	22/03/1917	28/03/1917

War Diary	Laundries Erquingham	29/03/1917	29/03/1917
War Diary	Bac. St. Maur	30/03/1917	31/03/1917
Miscellaneous	War Diary D.A.G. G.H.Q., 3rd Echelon.	07/05/1917	07/05/1917
War Diary	Bac St. Maur	01/04/1917	12/04/1917
War Diary	Trench Bois Grenier Sector	13/04/1917	20/04/1917
War Diary	La Rolanderie	21/04/1917	28/04/1917
War Diary	Trenches Bois-Grenier Sub-Sector	28/04/1917	01/05/1917
War Diary	Reference Trench Map France Sheet 36 N.W. Edition Y.A. 1/20000	02/05/1917	02/05/1917
War Diary	Trenches Bois Grenier Sub Sector	02/05/1917	06/05/1917
War Diary	Streaky Bacon Fm	07/05/1917	07/05/1917
War Diary	La Rolanderie Fms Near Erqvinghem	08/05/1917	14/05/1917
War Diary	Trenches Bois Grenier Sub Sector	14/05/1917	17/05/1917
War Diary	Trenches Bois Grenier Sector Flamengrie S.S	18/05/1917	22/05/1917
War Diary	Streaky Bacon	23/05/1917	23/05/1917
War Diary	Streaky Bacon	26/05/1917	26/05/1917
War Diary	La Rolanderie Fms	26/05/1917	26/05/1917
War Diary	Streaky Bacon	27/05/1917	27/05/1917
War Diary	La Rolanderie Fms	28/05/1917	30/05/1917
War Diary	In Trenches Bois Gremer Sector	30/05/1917	30/05/1917
War Diary	Flamengrie SS	31/05/1917	31/05/1917
Heading	War Diary Of 2/10th (Scottish) Battn The King's (Liverpool Regiment) Period 1st January 1917 To 30th June 1917		
War Diary	Bois Grenier Flamangerie Sub Sector Map Reference 36 N.W.4 7A	01/06/1917	07/06/1917
War Diary	Farm At H.17.d.4.3 La Rulanderie 2 Canteen Farms	08/06/1917	14/06/1917
War Diary	Farm At H.17.d.4.3. Canteen Farms La. Rolanderie Map Refernce 36 N W 4 7 A	15/06/1917	20/06/1917
War Diary	Erquingham	21/06/1917	27/06/1917
War Diary	Bois Grenier Flamangerie Sub Sector Map Reference 36 N W 4 7a	28/06/1917	30/06/1917
Miscellaneous	172nd Infantry Brigade 57th Division	30/06/1917	30/06/1917
War Diary	Bois Grenier Flamangerie Sub Sector Map Reference 36 N W 4 7 A	01/07/1917	08/07/1917
War Diary	Farm At H.17.d.4.4 La Rolanderie Farm Factory At Erquinghem	09/07/1917	18/07/1917
War Diary	Bois Grenier Rue Du Bois Sub-Sector Map Reference 36 N W 4 7 A	19/07/1917	26/07/1917
War Diary	Erquingham	27/07/1917	31/07/1917
Heading	2/10 Liverpool Vol 7 War Diary 2/0		
War Diary	Erquingham	01/08/1917	03/08/1917
War Diary	Bois Grenier Rue Du Bois Sub. Sector Map Reference 36 N.W.4 7 A	04/08/1917	12/08/1917
War Diary	Erquingham	13/08/1917	20/08/1917
War Diary	Bois Grenier Rue Du Bois Sub. Sector Map Reference 36 N W 4 7 A	21/08/1917	28/08/1917
War Diary	Erquingham	29/08/1917	31/08/1917
Heading	War Diary 2/10 Jun Lpool		
War Diary	Erquingham	01/09/1917	05/09/1917
War Diary	Bois Grenier Rue Du Bois Sub Sector Map Reference 36 N.W.4 7 A	06/09/1917	13/09/1917
War Diary	Erquinghem	14/09/1917	17/09/1917
War Diary	Estaires	18/09/1917	18/09/1917
War Diary	Basrieux	19/09/1917	19/09/1917
War Diary	Flechin	20/09/1917	09/10/1917

War Diary	Coin Perdu Proven	18/10/1917	25/10/1917
War Diary	Elverdinghe	26/10/1917	01/11/1917
War Diary	Langemarck	02/11/1917	05/11/1917
War Diary	Elverdinghe	06/11/1917	07/11/1917
War Diary	Zutkerque	07/11/1917	06/12/1917
War Diary	Herzeele	07/12/1917	17/12/1917
War Diary	Elverdinghe	18/12/1917	19/12/1917
War Diary	Elverdinghe (Emile & Larry) Camps	19/12/1917	25/12/1917
War Diary	Canal Bank	26/12/1917	31/12/1917
War Diary	In The Field	29/12/1917	02/01/1918
War Diary	H.Camp (A.10.a.0.2)	03/01/1918	04/01/1918
War Diary	Hollebecque Camp	05/01/1918	12/01/1918
War Diary	Erquinghem	13/01/1918	17/01/1918
War Diary	Houplines Sector	18/01/1918	20/01/1918
War Diary	Houplines Sector Hollebeque Camp	21/01/1918	27/01/1918
War Diary	Houplines Sub Sector H.5.b.9.8.	28/01/1918	01/02/1918
War Diary	Houplines Sub Sector	01/02/1918	07/02/1918
War Diary	L' Epinette Sub Sector	08/02/1918	08/02/1918
War Diary	Armentieres Sub-Sector	09/02/1918	14/02/1918
War Diary	Neuf-Berquin Area	15/02/1918	28/02/1918
War Diary	Estaires Neufberquin Fleurbaix	01/03/1918	31/03/1918
Heading	57th Division 172nd Infantry Brigade Battalion Disbanded 30.4.18 War Diary 2/10th Battalion The King's Liverpool Regiment 1st To 30th April 1918		
War Diary	Estaires	01/04/1918	01/04/1918
War Diary	Haverskerque	02/04/1918	02/04/1918
War Diary	Doullens	03/04/1918	03/04/1918
War Diary	St. Leger	04/04/1918	05/04/1918
War Diary	Sombrin	06/04/1918	07/04/1918
War Diary	Famechon	08/04/1917	11/04/1917
War Diary	Sombrin Pas	12/04/1917	15/04/1917
War Diary	Henu	16/04/1917	20/04/1917
War Diary	Burbure	21/04/1917	21/04/1917
War Diary	Festubert	22/04/1917	26/04/1917
War Diary	Labourse	27/04/1917	28/04/1917
War Diary	Vaudricourt	29/04/1917	30/04/1917
Heading	16th Division 47th Infy Bde 2-10th King's L'pool Regt		
War Diary	Vaudricourt	01/05/1918	01/05/1918
War Diary	Allouagne	02/05/1918	03/05/1918
War Diary	Neuf-Manoir	04/05/1918	13/05/1918
War Diary	Desvres	14/05/1918	17/05/1918
War Diary	Parenty	18/05/1918	23/05/1918
War Diary	Bezinghem	24/05/1918	30/05/1918
War Diary	Hesdin L'Abbe	31/05/1918	31/05/1918
War Diary	Chateau L'Enfer (5 C.61.8.5.)	01/06/1918	29/06/1918
War Diary	Map Ref Calais 13 1/100,000 Chateau L'enfer	30/06/1917	30/06/1917
Miscellaneous	2/10th (Scottish) Bn., King's Liverpool Regt.		
Miscellaneous	War Diary For Month Of July 1918	21/08/1918	21/08/1918
War Diary	Chateau	01/07/1918	01/07/1918
War Diary	Hovret (Map ref Calais 13 5 C.61.85)	05/07/1918	31/07/1918
War Diary	Etaples	04/07/1918	04/07/1918
Heading	57th Division 172nd Infy Bde 2-4th Sth Lancs Regt 1915 Sep-1916 Feb And Feb 1917-May 1919		

WO 95 2965/6

57 Divn; 172 Inf Brig
2/10 King's Liverpool Regt
1917 Feb - 1918 July

2/LS February, supplementary,
1917 rec with many diary

WAR DIARY of 2/10 (SCOTTISH) Kings (Liverpool) Regt

Army Form C. 2118

INTELLIGENCE SUMMARY

(Erase heading not required.)

Place	Date	Hour	Summary of Events and Information	Remarks and references to Appendices
BLACKDOWN BARRACKS	30.1.17		Lieut A.S. Darroch left for Divisional Duty at HAVRE as assistant Disembarkation Officer.	
— " —	1.2.17	7.50AM	Advance Party consisting of 5 Officers (Capt E.W.Bird, Capt R.H.Parkinson, 2/Lieut J.J.McGilvray (Commandant), 2/Lieut D.Hornand, 1st Lieut P.Kennelly) and 14 O.R. left to entrain at FRIMLEY STATION for FOLKESTONE	
FOLKESTONE	—	2 pm	Sailed for BOULOGNE	
BOULOGNE	—	4 pm	Arrived & disembarked immediately. Proceeded to a Rest Camp	
— " —	2.2.17		Rest Camp	
— " —	3.2.17	10 AM	Officers entrained for BAILLEUL (Remainder of party following next day). Delayed 7½ hours at CALAIS.	
HAZEBROUCK		11.5/a	Arrived & slept night	
— " —	4.2.17	AM	Proceeded on journey to BAILLEUL Met by motor lorries & taken to Bde Hqrs (ANZ Bde) BOIS GRENIER SECTOR. Where guides were provided to take on to Trenches	
BOIS GRENIER TRENCHES	4.2.17 11.2.17		Attached to A Coys out Comp of the 2nd Battn Canterbury Regt N.Z.E.F. N.C.Os where of advance Party joined up on the 11.5.2.17	
ERQUINGHEM	11.2.17 15.2.17		Rest	
BOIS GRENIER TRENCHES	16.2.17 19.2.17		Attached to 1st Battn C.I. Regt	

1875. W. W593/826 1,000,000 4/15 I.B.C.&A. A.D.S.S./Forms/C. 2118.

WAR DIARY 4 2/10 "C/Mid" Kings (Liverpool Reg.) Army Form C. 2118

INTELLIGENCE SUMMARY

(Erase heading not required.)

Instructions regarding War Diaries and Intelligence Summaries are contained in F. S. Regs., Part II. and the Staff Manual respectively. Title Pages will be prepared in manuscript.

Place	Date	Hour	Summary of Events and Information	Remarks and references to Appendices
TRENCHES BOIS GRENIER	18.2.17		Advance Party. During evening a N.L. patrol went out in front 2nd Batt McGilvray + Sergt Tyson accompanied it. The patrol encountered a strong patrol of about 15 men, + were bombed to same, Only two men of Patrol returned both wounded. Search was made, but no trace of remainder of party could be found. 2nd Lieut McGilvray + Sergt Tyson reported as "Missing believed Wounded"	Appx
—	19.2.17			
—	20.2.17		The 2nd Batt R.I. Regt relieved and Advance Party came out	Appx
ERQUINGHEM	21.2.17		Rest.	
—	22.2.17		Officers + N.C.O.'s of Advance Party visited the Left Batta Sector of the Brigade in Bois Grenier.	Appx
—	23.2.17		Bttn Marched to ESTAIRES + joined up with Transport Details of the Battn.	
TRENCHES BOIS GRENIER	27.2.17		2nd Lieuts A A FINNIGAN + J D EASTON (A + S Highlanders) reported for duty with Battn.	Appx

2/6.5. 26 January 1917.

WAR DIARY of 2/10" (Scottish) Kings (Liverpool) Regt

INTELLIGENCE SUMMARY

(Erase heading not required.)

Army Form C. 2118

Instructions regarding War Diaries and Intelligence Summaries are contained in F.S. Regs, Part II. and the Staff Manual respectively. Title Pages will be prepared in manuscript.

Place	Date	Hour	Summary of Events and Information	Remarks and references to Appendices
BLACKDOWN BARRACKS	16.2.17	7.30 AM	Transport + Details viz. 3 Officers (Major H H Maxwell, Capt E M Duckworth, Lieut A Jowett) and 83 Other Ranks, 64 Animals, 18 wheeled vehicles + 2 2-wheeled vehicles left to entrain at Frimley Station.	
SOUTHAMPTON		Noon	Arrived at SOUTHAMPTON	
		4.30 pm	Embarked on Transport ship "KARNAK"	
		6 pm	Left Dock. Escort of 2 Destroyers. Some Heavy rain during night. Some fog. Smooth Sea.	
HAVRE	17.2.17	6 AM	Arrived at Bar. Anchored till 5 pm	
		7 pm	Landed. Animals + vehicles disentrained by 8.30 pm. Men & remainder - Shed all night.	
HAVRE	18.2.17	7.30 AM	Left the Docks - marched to POINT 3 - Commenced entraining at once immediately on arrival about 8.30 AM Transport + Details of 2/4th Batt K.L.R. joined up on same train. Lieut. A.E. Barroch joined up on completion of duties - Remained with disembarkation of the Division.	
BLACKDOWN BARRACKS		11 AM	Remainder of Battn. left to entrain at FRIMLEY STATION	
SOUTHAMPTON		3 PM	— arrived. Held up by fog.	
BAILLEUL	19.2.17	3 pm	Transport etc arrived + detrained immediately. Marched about 6 miles to Billeting Area at SEC BOIS arriving 8.15 pm. Billeted - a farm. All Animals in good condition. Weather damp + misty	
SOUTHAMPTON			Rem. of Battn. Held up by fog.	

WAR DIARY of 2/10 (Scottish) King's (Liverpool)

INTELLIGENCE SUMMARY

(Erase heading not required.)

Instructions regarding War Diaries and Intelligence Summaries are contained in F. S. Regs, Part II. and the Staff Manual respectively. Title Pages will be prepared in manuscript.

Place	Date	Hour	Summary of Events and Information	Remarks and references to Appendices
BLACKDOWN BARRACKS	16.2.17	7.30 AM	Transport + Details, viz. 3 Officers (Major W.H. Maxwell, Capt E.H. Duckworth + Lieut A. Sowerby) and 23 other Ranks, 64 Animals, 18 Wheeled Vehicles + 4 Wheeled Vehicles left to entrain at Frimley Station.	
SOUTHAMPTON		Noon	Arrived at Southampton.	
		4.30 pm	Embarked on Transport Ship "Karnak"	
		6 pm	Left Dock. Escort of 2 Destroyers. Blew very hard during night. Down fog. Much Sea	
HAVRE	17.2.17	6 AM	Arrived at Bar. Anchored till 5 pm	
		9 pm	Landed, Animals + vehicles disembarked by 8.30 pm. Men & remainder & shed all night	
HAVRE	18.2.17	7.30 AM	Left the Docks + marched to Point 3 + commenced entraining between Transport + Details of 2/10 Batt. K.L.R. on arrival at 8.20 AM. Train & Lieut. A.S. Barroch joined us on completion of duties – connection with disembarkation of the Division.	
BLACKDOWN BARRACKS		11 AM	Remainder of Battn left to entrain at Frimley Station	
SOUTHAMPTON		3 PM	Arrived. Held up by fogs.	
BAILLEUL	19.2.17	2 pm	Transport etc arrived + detrained immediately. Marched about 2 miles to Billeting Areas at Sec Bois. Arriving 8.15 pm. Billeted – a farm. All animals in good condition. Weather damp + twisty.	
SOUTHAMPTON			Remr of Battn. Held up by fog	

WAR DIARY or INTELLIGENCE SUMMARY

Army Form C. 2118

of 2/10th (Scottish) Kings (Liverpool) Regt

Instructions regarding War Diaries and Intelligence Summaries are contained in F.S. Regs., Part II. and the Staff Manual respectively. Title Pages will be prepared in manuscript.

(Erase heading not required.)

Place	Date	Hour	Summary of Events and Information	Remarks and references to Appendices
SEC-BOIS	20.27	11am	Brigadier + Brigade Major called, + gave various instructions + orders + then accompanied to personal Brigade Hqr at BORRE. Weather wet.	
SOUTHAMPTON			Remr of Battn still held up by fog	
SEC-BOIS	21.27		Orders received from Brigade Hqr to move on following day to new billetting Area at OUTERSTEEN. Weather damp throughout.	
SOUTHAMPTON		4.30pm	Regt of Battn sailed on following Transport Steamers 1/3/28 CONNAUGHT Hqr. 12.47am 350.02 (on D.Pay) Officers Entrained { Lt Col A YOUNGE Capt + Adj DD FARMER & Lt. G.N. STANSBRIDGE " DONEGAL 9 -- (on D.Pay) Capt N.W. KIRSTON RAMC Lieut E. COOKSON (Signalling Officer) " LYDIA 5 -- 90.08 Capt Rev: STEPHENSON (Padre) Capt A.B HOWDEN A Co Major R.H.D. LOCKHART, B.C. Capt W DAVIDSON Capt A McD DOUGHTY Lieut G.M. MORRIS 2ⁿᵈ Lieut J.C. BELFORD J. SILAVAN " J. FILSHIE " D. SMITH (Cameron Hdrs) " R.J. McKINNEN C Co Capt A.P. DICKINSON D Co Capt A COOKSON Lieut L. BARNISH Lieut T.A ROBERTS 2ⁿᵈ - J.H MGNNIE 2ⁿᵈ Lieut E.E EDGAR " - W SARGENT (Cameron Hdrs) " J.A FULTON (Cameron Hdrs) " - J DARROCH " W FAIRCLOUGH (6ᵗʰ K.L.R)	

WAR DIARY of 2/1ᵘʳ (Scott.) (S) Kings (Liverpool) Regt.
or
INTELLIGENCE SUMMARY
(Erase heading not required.)

Army Form C. 2118

Instructions regarding War Diaries and Intelligence Summaries are contained in F.S. Regs, Part II. and the Staff Manual respectively. Title Pages will be prepared in manuscript.

Place	Date	Hour	Summary of Events and Information	Remarks and references to Appendices
SEC BOIS	20.1.17	11 AM	Brigadier & Brigade Major called, & gave various instructions & handed over orders & new documents for perusal. Brigade HQrs at BARRE, Weather Wet.	NIL
SOUTHAMPTON			Remvd Batta. Still held up by fog	
SEC-BOIS	21.1.17		Orders received from Brigade HQrs to move on following day to new Billeting Area at QUAESTERSTEEN. Weather damp Windy.	
SOUTHAMPTON	4 P.M.		Remr Batta. Sailed on Hunsary Transport Steamers (at Convalescent Hosps.12th Hussars 350, OR (am. Bay))	
			Officers Embarked: { Lt. Col. A. FAIRRIE, Capt. & Adj. D.D. FARMER v.c. Lt.& Qr CLAREBRIDGE, ½ DONEGAL 9 -- Major	
			Capt. J.H. KIDSTON RAMC, Lieut. E. COOKSON (Signalling Officer) 28 INDIA 9 -- Capt. & Sub.	
			Capt. ROW STEPHENSON (Padre) Capt. H.B. HOWDEN 5 -- 2nd Lt	
				90 OR.
			A Coy. Major R.H.S. LOCKHART B.C. Capt. W.N. DAVIDSON	
			Capt. J.W. McD DOUGALTY Lieut. G.M. MORRIS	
			2nd Lieut. J.C. BELFORD J SILLAVAN	
			J FILSHIE 2nd Lt D SMITH (Cameron Hrs)	
			R.J. McKINNELL	
			C Coy. Capt. A.P. DICKINSON D Coy. Capt. A. COOKSON	
			2nd Lt. L. BARNISH Lieut. T.H. ROBERTS	
			— J.A. McGHIE 2nd Lieut. G.E. EDGAR	
			— W. SARGEANT (Cameron Hrs) — J.A. FALTON (Cameron Hrs)	
			— S. DARROCH — W. FAIRGRIEVE (a KLR)	NIL

99

WAR DIARY of 2/10 (Scottish) King's (Liverpool) Regt

Army Form C. 2118

INTELLIGENCE SUMMARY

(Erase heading not required.)

Place	Date	Hour	Summary of Events and Information	Remarks and references to Appendices
Sec Bois	22.2.17		Orders to move to OUTTERSTEEN Cancelled. Transport etc ordered to move on the 23rd inst to ESTAIRES Area. Weather damp & misty	
HAVRE		6 AM	Remy Battn arrived & after disembarking marched to POINT 3 and entrained	
		3 pm	Left POINT 3	
Sec Bois	23.2.17	11 AM	Transport etc left for ESTAIRES arriving 3 pm. Went into Billets there.	
BAILLEUL		10.30 pm	Remy Battn arrived.	
		11.15	Marched off to ESTAIRES. (about 9 miles) arrived 3.30 AM	
ESTAIRES			Orders received to take over Trenches in Bois GRENIER Sector on Monday 26.2.17. Kit Inspection. Lecture by Divisional gas officer on use of it's Small Box Respirator.	
ESTAIRES	24.2.17	10 AM	Small Box Respirators issued to Battn & tested at Divisional Gas School. Party of officers & NCOs Proceeded to Trenches, Bois GRENIER Sector (about 8 miles distant) occupied by 2nd Canterbury Regt N.Z. Division, preparatory to taking over. Weather fine. (Col Stewart)	

(2nd ARMY. ANZAC Army Corps)

WAR DIARY of 2/10 (Scottish) King's (Liverpool) Regiment

INTELLIGENCE SUMMARY

(Erase heading not required.)

Army Form C. 2118.

Instructions regarding War Diaries and Intelligence Summaries are contained in F.S. Regs., Part II. and the Staff Manual respectively. Title Pages will be prepared in manuscript.

Place	Date	Hour	Summary of Events and Information	Remarks and references to Appendices
Sec Bois	22.2.17		Orders for move to OUDTERSTEEN cancelled. Transport etc ordered to move on the 23rd inst to ESTAIRES Area. Weather damp & misty	
HAVRE		6 AM	Remr Battn arrived & after disembarking marched to POINT 3 and entrained	
		3 pm	Left POINT 3	
Sec Bois	23.2.17	11 AM	Transport etc from ESTAIRES arriving 3 pm Went into Billets there	
BAILLEUL		10.30 pm	Remr Battn arrived.	
		11.15	Marched off to ESTAIRES (about 9 miles) arrived 3.30 AM	
ESTAIRES			Orders received to take over trenches in BOIS GRENIER Sector on Monday 26.2.17 Air Inclusive Lecture to Divisional Gas officer on use of a Small Box Respirator	
ESTAIRES	24.2.17	10 AM	Small Box Respirators issued to Battn & tested at Divisional Gas School Party of officers & NCOs proceeded to trenches, BOIS GRENIER sector (at this time occupied by 2nd Canterbury Regt. N.Z. DIVISION preparatory to taking over. Weather fine (C.F. Gosward's)	

(2nd ARMY. ANZAC. ARMY CORPS)

WAR DIARY
INTELLIGENCE SUMMARY
(Erase heading not required.)

Army Form C. 2118

2/10th (Scottish) Kings (Liverpool) Regt.

Instructions regarding War Diaries and Intelligence Summaries are contained in F. S. Regs., Part II. and the Staff Manual respectively. Title Pages will be prepared in manuscript.

Place	Date	Hour	Summary of Events and Information	Remarks and references to Appendices
TRENCHES ESTAIRES. TRENCHES. BOIS GRENIER Ref: TRENCH MAP BOIS GRENIER 36 NW 4 Part 6 D Scale 1:10000	26.2.17	8 AM	Battn left for Trenches. Strength 30 Officers 836 O.R. to relieve 2nd Canterbury Regt. NZ Divn. Fine bright day. (QM Stores + part of Transport moved to ERQUINGHEM Rear Transport Brigade billetted near SAILLY	
		NOON	Relief commenced	
		2:30pm	Relief completed.	
			172nd Brigade holding LEFT Sector of Divisional Frontage 171st Brigade CENTRE 174th Brigade RIGHT (AUSTRALIAN Division on LEFT 56th Division on RIGHT)	
			Battn holding RIGHT Sector of Brigade frontage (A Coy Right Distribution B Coy Left Front + Support line Q.R. Subsidiary line A	
			2/4 S.Lancs Regt LEFT HQr + between Subsidiary + support line	
			2/5 " Brigade Reserve only Lights held by 1 Platoon in Rjwr, 2 on left	
			2/9 K.L.R. Divisional Reserve FRONT LINE Held in addition I 26.C.2.2 Inclusive	
			Battn FRONTAGE from I 31.8.4.4. to I 26.C.2.2 Inclusive	
			Intermittent Shelling H.E. + Minnies during afternoon + evening	
	9.40-10pm	Heavy Bombardment by enemy on left of Brigade Sector		
	12.30 AM	Second Some retaliation on our front after Bombardments (Road by AUSTRALIAN Regt)	AAAA
			Casualties 2/OR (one slightly wounded one NCO wounded. Shell-Shock.)	
	27.2.17		A number of Minnies + Some H.E. over at intervals during day, otherwise quiet	
			Weather Fine	AAAA
			Casualties NIL	
	28.2.17		About noon Several Minnies landed in our left Sector near parapet one man killed + one officer (Lieut McKinnell) stunned. MTM Battery fired a minute of rounds	
			Some shelling in afternoon fairly heavy shelling between 10 & 11 pm about which time heavy bombardment heard some miles to NORTH. One or two Rurfocks? Gas Shells fell near Battn HQrs.	
			Casualties 1 Pte killed 1 wounded Shell-Shock	AAAA

WAR DIARY 2/10th (Scottish) Kings (Liverpool Regt)

INTELLIGENCE SUMMARY

Army Form C. 2118

(Erase heading not required.)

Place	Date	Hour	Summary of Events and Information	Remarks and references to Appendices
Trenches Estaires	26.2.17	8 AM	Batln left for Trenches. Strength 30 offrs 836. O.R. to relieve 2nd Canterbury Regt NZ Div Fine bright day (QM Stores & Baln Transport moved to E.R.DUNKERLEY Regt Transport SAILLY	
Trenches Bois Grenier (Rep. Trench Map Bois Grenier 36 N.W. 4 Edn 6.D Sult. I. 1000)		NOON	Relief commenced.	
		2·30 PM	Relief completed.	
			172nd Brigade holding LEFT Sector of Divisional front. Capt. 171st Brigade CENTRE 170th Brigade RIGHT (AUSTRALIAN DIVISION on LEFT 56th Division on RIGHT)	
			Batln holding RIGHT Sector of Brigade frontage (A Coy RIGHT Distribution 24 R's Lancs Regt LEFT (B Coy LEFT Avenity Support Wn C D Sections in 2nd 2/5 " " Brigade Reserve (Agr Helestown So Buildings only 2nd Before on Right 2 on Left 2/9 M.R. Divisional Reserve FRONT LINE to T 26 c 2.2 inclusive RIGHT FRONTAGE from T 31 c 4.4 to T 26 c 2.2 inclusive	
	27.2.17	9·40-10 PM	Intermittent shelling H.E + Minnies during afternoon or evening Heavy bombardment by our Guns on left of Brigade Sector	
		10·30 AM	Second _____ _____ on our front. (After These Bombardments (Raid by AUSTRALIAN Regt) possible Bn (one slightly wounded one NCO wounded-Shell Shock)	
			Casualties a minute of Minnies + some H.E. over at intervals during day, otherwise Quiet Heather Line Casualties N.I.L	
	28.2.17		About 10 PM several 'Minnies' landed in our Left Sector, near Trenchet two men killed, one officer (Lieut McKinnell) stunned. H.V. Battery fired a number of rounds two our Sector to afternoon. Forty Hang Shelling between 10 & 11 PM about which two heavy Bombardment fired some miles to NORTH one or two Searchlights on Enemy fell near Batln Hqrs	10/85
			Casualties 1 PTE KILLED Number R.J. SCHOFIELD	

WAR DIARY of 2/10th (Scottish) Kings (Liverpool) Regt

INTELLIGENCE SUMMARY

Army Form C. 2118

Place	Date	Hour	Summary of Events and Information	Remarks and references to Appendices
TRENCHES BOIS GRENIER	1.3.17	1 AM	Several shells fell close to QUEER STREET (Communication Trench from Bath Hgrs to White City) and near Hqrs about 4.30 AM. No damage. Night otherwise quiet. M.T.M. Battery fired about 100 Rounds from Front Line during afternoon. Some retaliation after on Left of Sector. A number of Hun aeroplanes seen in afternoon behind our lines. Fired on by Anti-Aircraft guns. Weather fine + bright. Casualties NIL.	AWN
	2.3.17		Quiet except morning. Morning Parties engaged on drainage trench & Communication Trench from Support to Firing Line (SAFETY ALLEY & STANWAY AV) MTM fired about 100 Rounds from Right of Sector in afternoon. Some retaliation from Hun without doing any damage. Casualties NIL	AWN
	3.3.17		Quiet night & fairly normal Vick. Artillery on Left Subs. Quiet all morning. Our guns fired about 100 Rounds HE + Shrapnel during afternoon at Bunkhing + road beyond, opposite Brigade Left Sector, which brought immediate retaliation. LTM shelled Hun wire & Bracket opposite Right Sector, when replied with Wizz-Bang on the Support Line, 9 or 10 falling about front line, New Queen Street + Moat Farm Av. Two HE Shells dropped close to Bath Hqrs, + one at a Strong Small Arms Rect Land from M.G.s. concentrated on Supply Depot at Hqrs. Le Bas Farm at from 6pm to 10.30pm. Patrols out at night in No Mans Land. No enemy met. Bright Moon Light. Casualties NIL. Major R.H.D. LOCKHART left in evening to take over Commandant Duties at Divisional Railway School	AWN

WAR DIARY of 2/10 (Scottish) Kings (Liverpool) Regt

INTELLIGENCE SUMMARY

Army Form C. 2118

Place	Date	Hour	Summary of Events and Information	Remarks and references to Appendices
TRENCHES. BOIS GRENIER	4/3/17		Quiet night. Reconnaissance made of our wire along front. Patrols out during night. Report barricade removed for repairs. F.S.D.! A few heavy shells lobbed in outskirts of Armentières with 5.9s RE. Very heavy firing by our Artillery all day. Retaliation to "Minnie" bombardment at 4.30 pm. Very effective. One of our Stoke[?] shells fell short landing in parapet of Bridoux Salient. No damage. Aeroplane patrols frequent. Two seen very high up in afternoon. M.Gs. Live at 4 Ruins concentrated on Enfilade Sector when at Le Bas Hill from 7.30 to 12.35 AM. Enemy Artillery quiet during morning, but 6 shots of HE on our Suburbian line & Girls School - Shell damage from active in afternoon. Some shrapnel & two HE shells burst in Vicinity of work in Bois Grenier. Trenches etc. CASUALTIES. NIL. (See below on other side for ammunition expended)	
	5/3/17		Quiet night. MMG Heavy swept during early hours of morning. Enemy TM's more active. Our Artillery registering all morning. Retaliation for afternoon & evening. M.Gs much as given. Fired a turn in Enemy line, which was immediately followed by flash in smoke of their Trenches. Hostile Enemy Artillery very active in afternoon. Practically no reply from our guns. All kinds of shells including gas. Gas shell started the lachrymatory had a low velocity made a peculiar noise passing over front line. They were sent with HE shells into region of Tramway Av New Queen's R Shells also fell near Crambabot Dump. Lachrymatory gas located in Bois Grenier. Gas alarm given at 6.30 pm and again about 8 pm (No man 26/3/9 B Coy) in Greatwood by Rochville Horn at [?], for about 10 minutes on each occasion. CASUALTIES. NIL.	

WAR DIARY of 2/10th (Scottish) King's (Liverpool) Regt

Army Form C. 2118

INTELLIGENCE SUMMARY
(Erase heading not required.)

Place	Date	Hour	Summary of Events and Information	Remarks and references to Appendices
TRENCHES BOIS GRENIER	6.3.17		Quiet night. Bright frosty morning.	
		11 AM	2/9th K.L.R. started Relief at 11 AM	
		1.5 pm	Relief Completed. Hun sent over considerable number of S.Lille H.E. Shrapnel during Relief, especially on Left Sub-Sector. One Shrap. HE slightly wounded 4 men. Casualties N.E.	
ERQUINGHEM			Battalion billeted in this area. HQr A + B Coys in farms about 1 mile South and D Coy in Welsh Town.	(Nil)
	7.3.17		Hard frost + strong Easterly wind. Battn. Pay + Rest + cleaning up. First Relief left for Lewis Gun Course at La Touquet.	(Nil)
	8.3.17		Saw front 9.15 to 12.30 Physical Drill Bayonet fighting etc. Orders to move to new Billets. Arms received. 2/Lt Bedford & Menzie Report for Course at Divisional Raiding School along with 20 ORanks.	(Nil)
	9.3.17		Major Maxwell, Lieut G.M. Morris + Fulton as Q.M. Sergt. Cross + 4 Cry Cooks proceeded to Hazebrouck for notes. Berry to inspect 2nd Army School of Cookery in the field. Lieut Schut of Cookery near Brigade HQrs. HQr, A + B Coys moved to Billets at Rolanderie Farm. Weather Frost + snow. Major Maxwell, C + D Coys to Billets at Rue Marle.	Nil
LA ROLANDERIE RUE MARLE	10.3.17		Close order drill. Short Route marches to Croutoups etc. Battalion now in Brigade Reserve. Brigade took over Relief of the Rue de Bois. Sector (from Grantham's avenue Bois Grenier Sector to Pear Tree Farm). Three Batt. in Trenches, one in Reserve. (Ref. Map Sheet 36 NW) Weather Fine + warmer.	Nil

WAR DIARY or INTELLIGENCE SUMMARY

Army Form C. 2118

4th Bn 21st (Central) Kings (Liverpool) Regt

Place	Date	Hour	Summary of Events and Information	Remarks and references to Appendices
LA ROMBERIE RUE MARLE	11/3/17		Church Parades morning. Hun Aeroplane over behind our lines about 1 p.m. Brought down one of our Balloons. Heavy firing all day by our Artillery — Nil "travelling fuses". Weather Fine & Clear. Warmer.	Nil
"	12/3/17		"C" Coy relieved A Coy 2/5th South Lancs Regt on Left 4 Battn new Sector (Bois Grenier) at 11 A.M. H.qrs A, B, & D Coys relieved 3 Coys of 2/4th Battn K.L.R. Marched from Billets a few S Bn Relief completed 8 p.m. H.qrs at Hd CARLETON near RATION FARM. Disposition A & R.H. Coys (Grenadier Avenue to Stanway) D Centre Sector (Stanway Av. to Kew Street) C in Street in Park with B Coy + D.R. 2/4 KLR in relay line. Casualties – Nil.	Nil
TRENCHES (BOIS GRENIER SECTOR)	13/3/17		Quiet day. Heavy Bombardment on Left 4 Brigade Sector between 11:30 & 1 A.M. Weather fine & hazy. Casualties - Nil	Nil
"	14/3/17		Quiet night. Communication Trenches (com. Right (Rmt of Mint Farm Avenue New Gutter & Straight Tce (?)) in very bad condition. Started repair work. Artillery own Intermittent fire during day. Some Heavies fell near Oyster Farm. Enemy Quiet most of day. A few H.E. fell on left & near Right of Centre Sector. Some shrap. M.G. Shrapnel fire on Bridge at Culvert Farm. T.M.B. — 6 pfr Minnies fell near Water + Flamengrie Farms. Weather Rain in morning + Late afternoon. Casualties 3. (O.Cm 1 Killed 1 Died of wounds 1 Shell Shocked)	Nil
	15/3/17		Quiet in front of our line Patrolled during night. Enemy patrol met at 11 P.M. & returned to their own lines. Patrolling difficult owing to darkness & state of No Mans Land. Our Artillery. Normal + Retaliatory fire. Six minnies registered on Bridge Fort + Water Samms ind. M.G. Normal firing directed on Hd Carp Notre d Lamouzie. Enemy Artillery. More active. Tramway entrance shelled also Bolton qrs about 25 H.E. at 4 a.m. Casualties 2 wounded (D.G.) at rear 'Tramway Avenue'. Weather fine + Clear.	Nil

WAR DIARY

2/10 (Scottish) Kings (Liverpool) Army Form C. 2118

INTELLIGENCE SUMMARY

Place	Date	Hour	Summary of Events and Information	Remarks and references to Appendices
TRENCHES (Bois GRENIER SECTOR)	14/3/17		Patrols out all night, no hostile patrols seen or heard. No Man's Land reported heavy firing between ? & left flank. 12.45 AM (Lieut L.J. GARROCH) to reconnoitre Enemy firing line & report. WIRE reported low. Enemy's MG's fairly hot. Weak & evenly covered. Our Artillery normal. In afternoon in registering several 18 pounders fell short, bursting in BALQUHE SALIENT. Considerable damage done to Enemy's trenches opposite our front. T.M.B.'s normal. T.M's been minnies fell in YORK, IVY & third LINES. Enemy to day active throughout day. Weather fine and sunny.	WEW
" "	17/3/17		Patrols Special Patrol of 6 O.R. Left our lines on Right of BALDOUR SALIENT at 7.30 → 9.40 pm. Leaving 0.20 & 11.45 respectively. Proceeded to within 20 yds Enemy front. Object hostile patrols having been reported in locality, to lie in wait. If possible. Get a prisoner. No hostile patrols encountered. On patrolling quiet. Retaliation Registering only. Normal. Pack Row locality & LIMITS STREET between H30 & Q30 am. Average active 2nd Rate S.R. KEIG, W.G. McLAREN F.H. HOLLINS MASHOOD, S. STEAD, S.W. MARSH, reported for duty with Battn. All from Reserve Battn. Infantry.	WEW
" "	18/3/17		Patrols sent patrolled during night & reported quiet. Our Artillery HE morning intermittent fire on Inskers & inconsistent trenches. Aircraft Six of our planes flew over Enemy lines in direction of train observation Balloon which was immediately hauled down. Enemy 4 hostile planes on return, not got through safely. Enemy Artillery active & accurate. Two Dug-outs behind T 26.4 & Bomb Store in T 26.2 destroyed. Whiz Bangs also at BALEGE GREEN & HE at TRAMWAY Rd Several "minnies" fell in JOCKS JOY. Aircraft Hostile planes attacking our observation Balloon, driven off. At 8.15 pm 5 Red Rockets fire on our left front. Our Artillery responded. CASUALTIES NIL	WEW

WAR DIARY of 2/14 (Scottish) Kings (Liverpool) Regt Army Form C. 2118

INTELLIGENCE SUMMARY

(Erase heading not required.)

Place	Date	Hour	Summary of Events and Information	Remarks and references to Appendices
TRENCHES BOIS-GRENIER SECTOR	19.3.17		Patrols out during night to examine our wire. Reported good in front of I.26.5. & fairly good between I.26.1 & I.22.1 Special Patrol 1 Officer (Lieut. S. Darroch) 1 Sergt 1 Cpl & 2 Prts. left our Trench 2 AM at J.31.d.20.65. (nr Bridoux Salient) intending to enter Enemy Trench at INCREASE BRIDGE to take a prisoner or obtain identifications. Enemy part of Harvey Patrol worked through their wire. German Sentry could be heard walking up down. Sounds of Whistling Lately could be heard & noise from Men in Trench. The Party advanced to ditch about 4 yds wide Separating them from Enemy Parapet. Sounds of Laughing & speaking became more evident, & as it was deemed trench was held & manned in strength & ground ditch untraced, Patrol withdrew & returned to our trench at 4.30 AM. Enemy showed much more alert. Rifle Grenades & Rifles into No Man's Land. A period of calm by our Artillery. The Shelling heavy CASUALTIES — 1 Pte (Bulley) killed & 1 Pte (Bierley) wounded (INCONSISTENT in any known CONTINUOUSLY SYSTEM when also shelled)	
			Enemy — Regt. before Junction to our trenches 20 W.N.B. Bavaria 4 HQr in SAFETY ALLEY (at I.37.3 to all Shrapnel Shells at front line trench. In afternoon 3 Salvos about front I.14.6.7 (Rue & Beaupre) A bund Shell fell in BRIDEAR NAVE M.C. relieved Pte of a new type 97.15.15 Sm long & 3 in. in diameter; piece very MG fire on hand Enfilade and mortal Shells 20 x Frounded for destructing from Near Exch. We did not have. Enfilade fire in rear near CALVERT FARM.	
	20.3.17		Patrol MacIntyre Henderson Patrol left I.26.1.20.95 to reconnoitre No Man's Land between I.26.d.5.3 + I.26.d.00.65 returned 1.25 AM No Man's Land reported Good grass. our Artillery active all day. Enemy — See active. Burst of Machine Gun fire from Shrapnel on front line, W Centre Company REGULARLY W.L.	
	21.3.17		Patrols Lukin MMH at intervals during night. No Enemy Patrol encountered Our Artillery fairly active during day. Especially about 4 pm. 2 M.T. Riel air bombs I.26.d.50.95 + I.36 bd.3 Enemy Bombardment Leaving to Enemy Bomber store Enemy & Artillery active between 12 Noon & 11 pm. Trench Mortars Quiet. MGun Quiet during day & night after Patrol & Hostile Planes flew over our lines at 4.20 returning shortly after. Relief 2/8 K.L.R from LA Plisanderie (RUE BIRGER Rd) relieved 2/10 BOARD K.L.R. Bois GRENIER Sub Sector. Relief completed 9pm CASUALTY Pte Clarke (wounded)	

WAR DIARY of 2/10 (Scottish) Kings (Liverpool) Regt

INTELLIGENCE SUMMARY

Army Form C. 2118

Place	Date	Hour	Summary of Events and Information	Remarks and references to Appendices
Trenches Bois Grenier Sub Sector	21/5/17		Special Patrol. Two Officers (Lieut A.S. Darroch & 2nd Lieut J. Darroch) 1 Serjeant 2 Corporals + 4 Privates left our Trench at I.31.b.95.65 at 7.30 p.m. and proceeded across No Man's Land. After crossing ditch about midway between the two trenches, Enemy, who appeared the very alert sent up 3 "Very" Lights + turned their m.n. fire. Patrol remained quiet for 15 minutes and then approached Enemy's wire at I.32.a.50.45 A gap was known but on leaving 1 Corporal and 4 Privates as a Covering Party Lieut. A.S. Darroch + J. Darroch Sgt. Morris + Corp'l Cameron (NCOs) entered Enemy Trench at 11.45 p.m. They found no occupants at this point, first point investigated was a disused dug-out, nothing found here. Enemy Trench in good condition + well revetted Patrol waited at point of entry in hope of capturing an Enemy patrol, but after waiting till 1.15 AM without success proceeded along Trench to left to try and surprise a Sentry Group. Voices were heard about 70 yds along in next bay + Patrol was challenged, but being able to reply patrol waited quietly until two Bombs were thrown, which burst within two or three yards, to may Casualty having a slight wound just below the left eye sustained by Lieut A.S. Darroch. Alarm having been raised footsteps and running in direction of Patrol from 17th Hanks. The Sentry, who was only 10 yds away was hunted and the Patrol withdrew, regaining own Trenches by 2.15 A.M. without any further Casualty, although fired at all the way across No Man's Land. The Patrol managed to secure a wire board from one of the Bays of Enemy's Trench, which was safely brought back.	WWW

WAR DIARY or INTELLIGENCE SUMMARY

Army Form C. 2118

1/1th 2/1th (Scottish) Kings (Liverpool) Regt

Place	Date	Hour	Summary of Events and Information	Remarks and references to Appendices
LA ROLANDERIE BILLETS	22/3/17		A draft of 28 O.R. arrived from Reserve Bn. Baths, Kit Inspections etc. Weather Heavy rain fell at times during day	
	23/3/17		Company Training. Close order drill, Bayonet fighting etc. Weather Hard frost	
	24/3/17		Company Training, route march. During the day Enemy endeavoured to interrupt some Howitzer guns situated about 200 yds from LA ROLANDERIE about 180 shells fell on area, the day, several falling within a few yards of guns positions but none were undamaged. Weather Cold & frosty	
	25/3/17		Church Parades at ERQUINGHAM "A" Coy returned "B" Coy on Saturday night ("B" Coy having been left in as 11th Bn. Argyll Southrs. Had not relieved 2/8/17)	
	26/3/17		Company Training & Route marches. Headquarter Runners from Bn. & H.Q.R. to Battalion Hd. Qr. Divisional Rifle Action recommenced. Militia Haxwell Capt. Bird, Lieut. Howard, Fleming & Finnegan Weather Wet & stormy	
	27/3/17		Company Training etc. Weather Frosty	
	28/3/17		Battn. marched from billets at LA ROLANDERIE & took over billets at ERQUINGHEM, about 2 mile East of ERQUINGHEM from 8th (Irish) K.L.R. Weather Cold. Some rain.	
ERQUINGHEM BILLETS	29/3/17		Battn. moved from Kennedies to billets at BAC ST MAUR. Army Reserve to 6th (King's Liverpool) R. Irish & D Coys in Town A, B, & C coys in Farms and the 55 Divn. (West Lanc) Brigade now a Divisional Reserve. Weather Very stormy	

WAR DIARY of the 2/10 (Scottish) Kings (Liverpool) Reg.

INTELLIGENCE SUMMARY

Army Form C. 2118

Place	Date	Hour	Summary of Events and Information	Remarks and references to Appendices
BAC ST MAUR	30/3/17	-	Billets. Company & Specialist Training	
-	31/3/17		Billets. Three Lumbargo's supplied working parties to Subsidiary line Trench. Companies Continued Battalion & Battalion training. 2/Lieuts. A.S. DARROCH & J.MENNIE (Cameron Highrs) attached Battn. from a small Patrol out in No Mans Land at night. Patrol received Enemy's wire, but were spotted on Enemy sending up several Very lights. Patrol was fired at when moving from their trench. On Trenches, 2/Lieut A.S. DARROCH being hit by a bullet in the foot. Otherwise no Casualties.	

WAR DIARY

D.A.G.
    G.H.Q., 3rd Echelon.

    Herewith War Diary concerning this unit for the month of April 1917, for retention please.

In the Field.   ....Lt Col
7th May 1917.   Commanding 2/10th(Scottish)Bn
                        King's Liverpool Regiment.

WAR DIARY of 1st & 2/1st (Wessex) Royal Engineers (Fortress) Regt.

Army Form C. 2118

INTELLIGENCE SUMMARY
(Erase heading not required.)

Vol 3

Place	Date	Hour	Summary of Events and Information	Remarks and references to Appendices
Bac St Maur	1/4/17		Billets. Batt. supplied Working Parties (3 Companies) In repair of existing Trenches & Construction of new trenches in The CORDONNERIE & BOUTILLERIE Sectors. Weather Cold & Stormy	
	2/4/17		Billets. Working Parties as on previous day. Classes of Instruction Platoon Commanders & N.C.O.'s Continued attended by A.M. Platoon Commanders Class. Instructors Maj W.H. MAXWELL & Lieut A MORRIS. Lewis Gun — Lieut A. JUWETT Physical Drill & Bayonet Fighting — T.A. ROBERTS Bombing — L. BARNISH Subjects Bombs — P. CARNELLY & J. SUTTON Weather Very Cold & Heavy Snow Storm in afternoon & during evening	
	3/4/17		Billets. Working Parties & Instructional Classes as on previous day Weather Snow Throughout night. Lasting till midday	
	4/4/17		Billets. Working Parties & Instructional Classes as on previous day	
	5/4/17		Billets. Working Parties & Instructional Classes as on previous day	

Ref. MAP FRANCE
SHEET 36 NW
Edn. 6.c.
1/20,000

Army Form C. 2118

WAR DIARY of the 2/10(Scottish) King's (Liverpool) Regt.
or
INTELLIGENCE SUMMARY

(Erase heading not required.)

Instructions regarding War Diaries and Intelligence Summaries are contained in F. S. Regs., Part II. and the Staff Manual respectively. Title Pages will be prepared in manuscript.

Place	Date	Hour	Summary of Events and Information	Remarks and references to Appendices
BAC ST MAUR	6/4/17		Billets. Working Parties as on previous day. Instructional Classes. Physical Drill. Bayonet fighting & Snipers dropped owing to requirements of working parties. Major E. L. RODDY (Cheshire Regt.) assumed Command of Battn. vice. Lt.Col. A FAIRRIE	WNun
	7/4/17		Billets. Working Parties & Instructional Classes as on previous day.	WNun
	8/4/17		Billets. Working Parties & Instructional Classes as on previous day.	WNun
	9/4/17		Billets. Working Parties & Instructional Classes as on previous day. Inspection of Cookery 2nd Army inspected kitchens & sheds of D Coy. Weather Cold. Snow in morning.	WNun
	10/4/17		Billets. Working Parties & Instructional Classes as on previous day. Weather. Cold & Stormy. Snow showers throughout day	WNun
	11/4/17		Billets. Working Parties & Instructional Classes as on previous day. Coy Commanders to Trenches in BOIS GRENIER Sector.	ANun

WAR DIARY 2/10 (Scottish) Kings (Liverpool) Regt

INTELLIGENCE SUMMARY

Army Form C. 2118

Place	Date	Hour	Summary of Events and Information	Remarks and references to Appendices
BAC ST MAUR	12/4/17		Billets taken over during the day by the 2/5 Bn L'pool K.L.R. Baths relieved 2/8 (Irish) K.L.R. in BOIS GRENIER Sector. Relief completed 1:30 AM 13th. Weather fine & clear. CASUALTIES: 1 Man (Sergt Pemberton) killed (Rifle bullet)	Nil
TRENCHES BOIS GRENIER SECTOR	13/4/17		Our Artillery fired few Retaliatory Live Guns were quiet. Aircraft. At 7.15 AM a Squadron of Seven machines appeared flying from rear of Enemys trenches & passed over our line as if returning from an enterprise.	Nil
	14/4/17		Enemy Artillery at 10:30 AM 30 small shells fell in BURNT FARM, between 2 & 3 from the BREWERY (BOIS GRENIER) also shelled BOIS GRENIER killed several Frenchmen. Weather fine. The day handsome or Casualties reported. 23. ORF reported from 3rd Res. Bn. The night was quiet. A high number of flares were sent up by the Enemy & on consisting of Chains of lights varying in numbers from 2 to 12. Patrols went out inspecting our wire NML patrolled from 11 pm to 2.30 am. Our Artillery (10 Shots) fired on Intermittent Trench otherwise quiet. Enemy " " fired a few 5.9s fell near artillery position in Hospice Farm. At 11 AM a few hits were made on the hull of Cemetery feet of damage. BREWERY (BOIS GRENIER) shelled again in afternoon. CASUALTIES: Wks Barry received a Minor 2 Cpl Snipers hrs at new wooden shelter 1 Seriously (Lance Cpl Whitehead died in hospital at EPIENIX. Later W 8 am) At 3.45 PM enemy started a heavy heavy bombardment on Soutz to RAILWAY Bois Grenier Sector, 10 Minute later 2 Rifle Grenades were fired Our Trenches were not damaged to this section. A large TM Bomb on extreme wing caused 4 casualties in Bay. Shown some Stokes & Rifle Grenades were found.	Nil
	15/4/17			Nil

Ref. map:
BOIS GRENIER Sheet 36 N.W. 4
Edition 2 1/10.000

WAR DIARY
or
INTELLIGENCE SUMMARY

Army Form C. 2118

(Erase heading not required.)

of 1st Bn 2/4th (Seaforth) Skinya (Wireshout) Regt

Place	Date	Hour	Summary of Events and Information	Remarks and references to Appendices
Trenches Bois Grenier Sector	13/4/17		**Our Artillery** Enemy rear lines shelled between 10 & 11 pm. **M.T.M.** fired at 12.30 pm in INCOMPLETE TRENCH from T26c & T26b producing retaliation. LTM's fired in Enquetin damaging Enemy wire - whole shots exploded. Patrols out — N.M.L. uneventful quiet.	WNW
	14/4/17		**Enemy Artillery** Retaliation from T.M. @ Officers GREEN, KIWI Av & Front Line. Following shells reported from Bde Line, 2nd Bde to THOMPSON BNTAYLOR to BOY WEFT & OTHER H/STONE IL H/TWELVE (ICIL) **Patrols** N.M.L. Patrolled from 12 Mn till 4 am by 2 offs & 8 ORs all NIGHT. N.L. Prise - wire repaired at T26c. **Our Artillery** Retaliatory fire only, otherwise extremely quiet. **H-M.T.N.** at 1.30 pm Short bursts not in accordance with programme. **Enemy Artillery** A few 77mm HE & Shrapnel on KIWI Street, Lozange between 10 & 11 on Salient at N62 the Shells were all Heavy. A gun fired this morning. Each time shown that gun fired a round of MACHINE entire & came from left. MG fired into our trench in vicinity of BRIDOUX SALIENT THIS gun only fired a few rounds & is a new gun in the Sector. **Patrols** Party been examining wire in front of INDEX & INCREASE fired up by I.T.G. Casual LTMS 2 men wounded. Bde BAMB in Support line & KIWI Street	WMW
	19/4/17	2.30am	Raid by party of 2nd Bn E.BORDER 111th Brigade. From Centre of our Sector. Zero was 2.30 am at that time a Heavy Barrage had opened up on Quine, Alias, Inking 35 Minaukii. Enemy Remained about 3 minutes after burst of Raiders succeeded in entering Enemy's Trench but were unable to like any prisoners casualties our Bn 2 Killed & 5 wounded. After so Raid a party of RAIDING Kings Carmelly searched N.M.L. for wounded they remained in one party near Enemys wire some hours - a triple party went to our wires after party had finished. Enemys Barrage during Raid destroyed to Bays in Support line & JOCK'S JOY. Our current It was opened in SHAFFERSBURY AV, Jo force & gun emp & gun was to some damage was done to trench beyond 4 left Centre Gaps its Barrage extended to ENEMY FARM and passed ten minutes after opening it was impossible to do in gaps when in D. & Lift Shelling from 3/8 to KIWI-WELLESLEY Av 1.03	WMW

1875 Wt. W593/826 1,000,000 4/15 J.B.C. & A. A.D.S.S./Forms/C. 2118.

WAR DIARY or INTELLIGENCE SUMMARY

Army Form C. 2118

2/10 (Scottish) Kings (Liverpool) Regt

Place	Date	Hour	Summary of Events and Information	Remarks and references to Appendices
TRENCHES BOIS GRENIER Sub Sector	18/4/17		**Patrols** Mr Offan & 3 others raided Left our Trench at I.31.b.65.60 marched along ditch running between the lines to about I.32.a.50.65. No enemy encountered. One Sentry group heard MNs reported in front Breastwork. Enemy wire at about I.31.d.7.7. Trench recruited 4 Sentry group & 4 ORs Left I.31.d 44 95. Obey saw Enemy wire at about I.31.d.9.0.6.0. Something was seen to crawl from there along to a Machine Gun fired from about I.31.d.90.60. Saw Certain Ruts. There was a dug out Bereft. Saw another dug out fired into Enemy Trench. Three men were certain Ruts. Three men were certain Ruts. **Our Artillery** fired MG in retaliation. M.G. 2750 rounds fired during night. **Enemy**" Increased activity. HE & Shrapnel on support line between TRAMWAY & SHAFTESBURY AVE and N/W of KIWI Street. Rifle Grenades fired actively during night. Enemy Trench Mortar appeared to be held more strongly than usual, increased activity pointed to a Relief taking place. Weather. Snow showers between 5.30 AM & 10 AM turning to rain	W/Mar
"	19/4/17		**Patrols** Two Officers Patrols out during night. One observed INCONSISTENT Trench held by Enemy Snipers about 100 yds apart. Three Snipers were observed. **Our Artillery** fired 5 ound silenced Enemy T.M. Fires. Several Casualties were apparently inflicted. **MGs** fired 1750 rounds during night at various Targets. **Enemy Artillery** Increased activity still apparent. Little damage done. Support Trenches received nut shots. Explosions behind Enemy's lines seen heard at intervals during Morning. **Casualties** 1 Man Wounded (Bullet in head Enemy from Safety Alley)	40Mar
"	20/4/17		**Our Artillery** Normal. **MGs** fired 1200 rounds indirect fire during night. **Enemy** " TRAMWAY IN PARK Row (rear trench) KIWI ETR (near dugouts) BURNT & RATION FARMS Shelled during the day. Aircraft active during late afternoon flying high. Relieved by 2/9 K.L.R Relief Completed by 11.30 pm	W/Mar

WAR DIARY
of the 2/10 (Scottish) King's (Liverpool) Regt.

INTELLIGENCE SUMMARY

Army Form C. 2118

Place	Date	Hour	Summary of Events and Information	Remarks and references to Appendices
LA ROLANDERIE	21/4/17		**Billets.** Draft of 62 O.Rs. reported. # This draft left 3rd Res. Baltn. January 19, 1917 & were subsequently attached to Pioneer Baltn. in PLOEGSTREET Area. Draft inspected by G.O.C. Div. & Canadian Brigadier.	W/u
	22/4/17		**Billets.** During the night a Special Patrol under Lieut. KEARNEY while investigating INCREASE TRENCH found two loop-hole plates outside Enemy wire, & brought them back.	W/u
	23/4/17		**Billets.** Company Training, Working Parties to Trenches etc.	W/u
	24/4/17		**Billets.** Company Training. Working Parties as on previous day. While working during the night in front line Trenches had one man killed (Pte. Williamson) & one wounded by Rifle Grenade. CASUALTY: 1 By	W/u
	25/4/17		**Billets.** Company Training. Working Parties as on previous day. 3 officers 2nd Lieuts. CRICHTON, ABLENCOWE & E.H. WOODHALL returned from 3rd Reg. Baltn.	W/u
	26/4/17		**Billets.** Company Training etc. Working Parties as on previous day.	W/u
	27/4/17		**Billets.** Company Training. Working Parties as on previous day. 2nd Lieut. W.R. HOOD left for ENGLAND on 10 Days Special Leave.	W/u
	28/4/17		**Billets.** Baltn. relieved 2/9 K.L.R. in Bois GRENIER, Relief commenced 9.30 p.m. & completed by 11.45 p.m. Major W.R. MAXWELL Class of Instruction for Platoon Commanders (Training) Platoon Commanders at ERQUINGHEM. 6 officers 10 N.C.Os.	W/u

WAR DIARY

of 2/10 (Scottish) Bn K.L. Regt.

INTELLIGENCE SUMMARY

(Erase heading not required.)

Army Form C. 2118

Instructions regarding War Diaries and Intelligence Summaries are contained in F. S. Regs., Part II. and the Staff Manual respectively. Title Pages will be prepared in manuscript.

Place	Date	Hour	Summary of Events and Information	Remarks and references to Appendices
TRENCHES BOIS-GRENIER SUB-SECTOR	28/4/17		Our operations:- Artillery. During time of relief the enemy opposite BOIS GRENIER SUB-SECTOR fired a Red "very light" about 10.15 p.m. This was taken to be a signal from our front line for the 2nd S.L.s our Artillery opened at immediately, which enemy retaliated very heavily resulting in our sustaining 3 men killed.	J.S.
	29/4/17		Enemy. A fighting patrol of the enemy (estimated strength 15.20) approached our wire at T.31.a.35.45 and was between 20 & 30 hands (sic) the majority of which fell in our wire and parapet. The party rapidly withdrew on being fired on. Snipers. Reports fired at in INCOME and INCREASE trenches. Aircraft. Normal "good weather activity".	J.S.
	28/4/17		Enemy operations. Artillery. Enemy retaliated to our fire between 10-15 p.m. and midnight with 7.7cm and 10.5 cms mainly on Support trenches. M.Gs. More active than usual.	J.S.
	29/4/17		Snipers. Sniping Post suspected at O.1.a.3.7. One of our Sentries was shot through the head while firing over parapet at T.31.c.3.4. Defences. Parapet repaired at I.>7.a.1.9. Aircraft. Active. Two machines ventured over our line but were driven off by our Anti-Aircraft Guns.	J.S.

Army Form C. 2118

WAR DIARY
of 1st Bn (1/10th Scottish) R.K.L. Regt.
INTELLIGENCE SUMMARY

(Erase heading not required.)

Instructions regarding War Diaries and Intelligence Summaries are contained in F.S. Regs., Part II. and the Staff Manual respectively. Title Pages will be prepared in manuscript.

Place	Date	Hour	Summary of Events and Information	Remarks and references to Appendices
BOIS GRENIER Sub-Sector	29/4/17		**General.** A change in the behaviour of the enemy has been noticed during the last 48 hours and his activity has increased considerably. The appears to be more definite aim in his artillery work and special targets are selected and shelled. O.Ts have been registered and in retaliatory fire has been more "studied". M.Gs and rifles have fired more than usual and snipers are suspected at several points. The above changes have been most noticeable in the BOIS GRENIER SUB-SECTOR. Efforts will be made during our "tour" to counteract this.	
	30/4/17		**Our Shelling.** Quiet during the night. **Artillery.** Quiet during the night. **Patrols.** A special patrol left our trench at 1-30 am with a view to entering INCREASE TRENCH. They were discovered and fired at by a working party of the enemy party consisting of about 30 men. The patrol lay up until daylight began to appear but no favourable opportunity presented itself. Other patrols whilst moving further heard at INCOME TRENCH at I 26 c 2.8.1 [?] sounds strengthened and raised – but the Trench Ramparts Repairs. **Aircraft.** Active all day. Emergency ground at 15.15 am fired to which two explosions were heard **General.** A considerable number of rifle grenades were fired and some cases of gas activity from I 31.6 Arle and hay act near wrecked enemy aeroplane in N.M.L. for 4 hrs.	

WAR DIARY
of the 2/10th (Scottish) Bn. K.L.R.
INTELLIGENCE SUMMARY

(Erase heading not required.)

Army Form C. 2118

Place	Date	Hour	Summary of Events and Information	Remarks and references to Appendices

Trenches BOIS-GRENIER Sub Sector	20/4/17		**Enemy Operations.**
			Artillery:- Enemy a/gun showed increased activity and engaged following targets in our sector:- mostly with guns of larger calibre, one gun located firing in direction of RAVINGHEM-LYS being 110's deflection I.14.b.8.2.
			  11.15 a.m. 7.7cms on I.31.5.
			  * 11.10 to 12.30 pm. 10.5cms. H.O. I.19.A.5.0 near Rue Plaff (E. CARLTON)
			  * 11.10 to 12.15 am. village funerée H.11.a central & H.5.c. 30.30. during Relay & GRIS POT were probably during INDEX and INCREASE Trenches, they appear to be waning M.G.
			  Sniping:- Active gun in INDEX and INCREASE Trenches, they appear to be waning M.G. leaflets.
			Mining. Enemy continues strengthening his wire all along this front. Quiet on by our Lewis guns at I.36.C.9.1. INCOME and INCREASE Trenches.
			Signals. At 5.30 am Morse was heard to be sounded in enemy lines opposite our front.
			Aircraft. Enemy plane reported down in flames in HOUPLINES SECTOR normal activity in our sector.
			T.Ms. A few pineapples during early morning inflicted 3 casualties.
			Defence work observed in INDEX C.T. apparently an M.G. emplacement.
			Casualties. 3 men killed, 2 wounded (shell exploding in Bgr Grant Room)
			General. we kept harassing the Hun day & night with rifle grenades and snipers, an answer to his "pineapples", and his resistance is apparently dying much to quite.	

1875 Wt. W593/826 W/1,020,000 4/15 J.B.C. & A. A.D.S.S./Forms/C. 2118.

WAR DIARY

of 2/10th (Scottish) Bn. K.L.R.

INTELLIGENCE SUMMARY

Army Form C. 2118

Vol 4

4 x
13 sheets

Place	Date 1917	Hour	Summary of Events and Information	Remarks and references to Appendices
TRENCHES BOIS GRENIER SUB-SECTOR. Reference:- Trench Map FRANCE Sheet 36 N.W. Edition 7A. 1/10000	13th May		**Enemy Operations.** Aeroplanes active all day, one machine flying very low well behind our lines appeared to be hit. As it crossed N.M.L flying very low. 2nd Lt R. ASTLEY joined *BIRMINGHAM* and was wounded by a piece of shell. Our casualties during last 24 hours:- 2nd Lt H. L. WHITE and 1 O.R. wounded by "pineapples". **Our Operations.** M.T.M's & L.T.M's. Confined shoot on I. 26. d. 6. 6 and on suspected snipers lair in INCREASE TRENCH did excellent work and appeared to be very effective. Enemy retaliation ineffective. **Snipers.** Enemy lairs in INCREASE TRENCH silenced with above shooting. **General.** Rifle grenades were fired intermittently into INCOME TRENCH where a working party were heard. About 150 sent into INCREASE and INDEX Trenches during 20 "pineapples" in retaliation. M.T.M's & L.T.M's fired on I. 32. c. 10. 45 and I. 31. d. 75. 55 at 6.30 pm with good results. **Enemy Operations.** **Artillery.** Early active during the day all was the quieter. 30 T.M. fired on 2/7 & 2/10 scots on our front line & supports, our support of KIWI ST, TRAMWAY AVE, & TEDDY'S by R.R. & W. Snipers kept quiet. Enemy lay out who had located several lairs. **Defence:** Fired in Travel on INCOME TRENCH was fired at during night was work observed on parapet & INCONSISTENT SUPPORT at Salient I. 32. a. 60. 05 and I. 32. a. 70. 30.	G.R.O G.R.O G.R.O

WAR DIARY
of 2/10 (Scott) Bn K.L.R.
INTELLIGENCE SUMMARY
(Erase heading not required.)

Army Form C. 2118

Instructions regarding War Diaries and Intelligence Summaries are contained in F.S. Regs., Part II. and the Staff Manual respectively. Title Pages will be prepared in manuscript.

Place	Date	Hour	Summary of Events and Information	Remarks and references to Appendices
BOIS GRENIER SUB-SECTOR	2nd May		**Enemy Operations (a/c)** Aircraft. Moderate activity, 3 machines, one of which was painted red, gave an interesting exhibition of flying & strafing over our trenches last evening at 7 pm. General. A String O.P constructed of bricks with two very obvious slits in it walks exists at I.32.b. 0710. The artillery are being put on to this target.	
	3rd	ellog	**Own Operations** M.T.M & L.T.M. fired on I.32.C.1075 & I.31.d 75.55 with good results also destroyed two snipers lairs in INCREASE TR. General. We continued our policy of harassing the enemy with rifle grenades by day & night. **Enemies Operations** Active retaliation to our T.M. shoot with 7.7 cms and 10.5 cms on our front lines supports in vicinity of KIWI ST, TRAMWAY AV. & TEDDY'S BURROW. Four casualties suffered and trench tramway damaged — General. Enemies activity with working parties at night is very noticeable; sounds indicating use of iron girders & corrugated iron sheets.	
	4 May		Our operations. M.T.M & L.T.M - Combined shoot did considerable damage	

Army Form C. 2118

WAR DIARY
of 2/10 Scottish Bn KLR
INTELLIGENCE SUMMARY

(Erase heading not required.)

Instructions regarding War Diaries and Intelligence Summaries are contained in F. S. Regs., Part II. and the Staff Manual respectively. Title Pages will be prepared in manuscript.

Place	Date	Hour	Summary of Events and Information	Remarks and references to Appendices
TRENCHES BOIS-GRENIER SUB SECTOR	4 May (Contd)		Our operations (Contd) to enemy wire at I 32 a.6.6 Enemies operations — Artillery - Fairly heavy retaliation to our T.M. strafe with 7.7 cm & 10.5 cm on front line, WATER FARM & STANWAY AV. BOIS GRENIER fairly heavy shelled, one casualty at CROIX BALOT FM SIGNALLING A small balloon heliotrope in colour with white basket shaped attached fell in N.M.L. during day, was discovered by night, its object was not ascertained.	
		Major B.G. Fenn reported for duty today.		
		10.45 pm	The enemy put up 3 red lights to which our guns replied (mistaking it our SOS) Enemy retaliated moderately heavily for about 45 mins. during which our fire also was continued no casualties were reported	
	5 May		A comparatively quiet day - Some new form of gas shells are reported to have been used by the enemy, from a L.T.M., a continuous stream of projectiles was observed affusing a hail of sparks - the following is a description of a dud :- 7.5 Regd. m.w. Gas shell - Fuse L W H Z dr Z B. '7B. Cage 250 mm long. Base 33 mm in depth note	

1875 Wt. W593/825 1,000,000 4/15 J.B.C. & A. '7B. A.B.S.S./Forms/C.2118.

WAR DIARY
INTELLIGENCE SUMMARY

of 2/10 Scottish 10th K.L.R.

(Erase heading not required.)

Army Form C. 2118

Place	Date	Hour	Summary of Events and Information	Remarks and references to Appendices
TRENCHES BOIS GRENIER SUB SECTOR	5 May (contd)		Six round holes at bottom, driving band 15mm wide, white metal note. 6 graves - Shell contains liquid - Comparatively innocuous, no serious results being reported - 2/Lt E J McElymont reported for duty (D. Coy)	
	6		Our operations Patrol A special patrol of 2 Officers + 10 O.R. left our trench at I.31.a.2.8. with the object of raiding the Enemies trenches at I.31.a.central - after getting through the enemy wire our patrol was discovered. Rifles + rapid fire being opened on them + after about 30 mins made another attempt. They were unable to effect their object to owing to the alertness of the Enemy and after bombing enemy post were compelled to withdraw. no Casualties. Enemy's Operations Comparatively quiet - Batt. relieved by 2/9 K.L.R. (B Coy 2/10 KLR - (B Coy 2/10 KLR remaining in our line). The relief was carried out without casualty and the 2/10 KLR Wilson (less B Coy) marched to naval Billets in STREAKY BACON & LA ROLANDERIE PMs	

WAR DIARY
of 2/10 Scott ?? for K.L.R.
INTELLIGENCE SUMMARY
(Erase heading not required)

Army Form C. 2118

Place	Date	Hour	Summary of Events and Information	Remarks and references to Appendices
STREAKY BACON FM & LA ROLANDERIE FMS.	7	May	Owing to unusual activity in trenches, the usual night working parties provided by two Coys were cancelled - usual training carried on -	
NEAR ERQUINGHEM	8	May	Usual training during day. A night working party provided by A Co 2/10 KLR was about to commence work near I 31..3 when our artillery opened in answer to SOS put up by RIGHT BATTN on the RIGHT - a heavy bombardment/was immediately opened by the BOSCHE looking for & found our front, were taken by Surprise & suffered 17 casualties (5 killed)	
"	9	May	Usual training by day. Working parties provided for front line at night -	
"	10	May	Considerable activity — enemy artillery. — One casualty suffered by Co in Sub. line 'C' Company relieved B Coy (less 4.0 KLR) in Subsidiary line —	
"	11	May	Major THIN temporarily attached to 2/5 KLR as 2nd in Command.	
"	12	May	Usual training and night working parties continued - 4 casualties (wounded) occurred during these days - one by our A.A. Boosche shell -	
"	13	May	Sunday. The usual services were held -	
"	14	May	2/10 KLR (less C.Co) relieved 1/9 KLR (less 1 Co remaining in Sub. line) in D Coy on left, A Centre, B on Right and C in Sub line - Relief completed without incident at 11.30 pm	

Bd IS GRENIER Lecter A.D.S.S./Forms/C.2118.
1875 Wt.W593/826 1,000,000 4/15 J.B.C. & A.

WAR DIARY
of 2/10 Scottish BnKLR
INTELLIGENCE SUMMARY

Army Form C. 2118

(Erase heading not required.)

Place	Date	Hour	Summary of Events and Information	Remarks and references to Appendices
TRENCHES BOIS GRENIER SUB SECTOR	May 14		Two (2) casualties wounded caused by enemies pineapples.	
"	May 14		2/Lt J Dale (A Coy) and 25 O.R. (18 A.Coy + 7 D Coy) joined for duty.	
"	"	15	Our operations Artillery Very quiet. M.T.M - fired on INCOMPLETE T.R. & INCONSISTENT SUPPORT with good effect and without receiving retaliation. L.T.M. - A special stokes kept near BRIDOUX SALIENT for the purpose of affording immediate retaliation against enemies pineapples proved very successful. ENEMIES OPERATIONS The inactivity of the enemy artillery during past 24 hours has been very marked. Five (5) minor casualties occurred today by rifle grenades and pineapples. 14 O.R. joined for duty (6- A Co, 3 B Coy, 2 "C" Coy + 3 "D" Coy)	
"	16		Our operations - Very quiet. ENEMIES OPERATIONS - In the early hours of the morning about 8 of the enemy visited our trench and attacked our trench patrol (with whom was Capt Doughty third runner) at about I.26.D.3.2. but were quickly driven off. Although our	

1875 Wt. W5937/326 1,000,000 4/15 J.B.C. & A. A.D.S.S./Forms/C. 2118.

WAR DIARY
of 2/10 Scottish Rif KLR
INTELLIGENCE SUMMARY
(Erase heading not required.)

Army Form C. 2118

Place	Date	Hour	Summary of Events and Information	Remarks and references to Appendices
TRENCHES BOIS GRENIER SUB SECTOR	May 16 (cont)		Party was taken by surprise while traversing an unoccupied gap and a number of bombs were thrown by the enemy from previously chosen positions we suffered no casualties. - A search of the ground that showed that the Germans left no casualties in our hands. Several stick bombs and a cap were however obtained. Save for this the day/night passed very quietly.	
	May 17		Our operations Artillery – nothing special of interest – very quiet. Enemy operations Artillery Very quiet indeed. TM's more active, three positions active opposite this subsector. Other. At 1.30 am a hostile patrol appears to have approached on line at I.32.1. as two bombs were thrown near a sentry, but nothing was seen of the enemy who apparently withdrew immediately. Casualties One sentry killed – General. Our rifle grenadiers were active as usual especially during the night. – Usual work digging trench repairs carried on by us.	

WAR DIARY
2/10 Scottish or 10th K.L.R.
INTELLIGENCE SUMMARY
(Erase heading not required.)

Army Form C. 2118

Place	Date	Hour	Summary of Events and Information	Remarks and references to Appendices
TRENCHES. BOIS GRENIER S BOIS. FLEURBAIX S.S	May 18		**Our operations** Artillery - Quiet during night & morning - active during afternoon - chiefly in retaliation. **Enemy's operations** Artillery - During the day there has been intermittent shelling of front line & support. TOCKS JOY especially receiving attention. Retaliation afforded by us 4.5" How. was quick and effective - The enemy chiefly confined his attention to back areas - ERQUINGHEM BATHS were shelled and owing to damage to machinery have had to be closed - Two barges in river near outer River LYS were sunk. 2nd Lt BELFORD was wounded at the BATHS. 2nd Lt SMITH was wounded in FRONT LINE. **Aircraft**: At 5.50 pm two enemy aeroplanes made an attack on one of our observation balloons - they missed their mark. The occupants escaping in parachutes from the balloon - One machine returning very low over our own lines was attacked by our L.Gs & rifles, but regained his lines in safety. **Movement**. Enemy was very active last night & this (early) morning all along his front with working parties, heavy transport and engine whistles were also heard.	

WAR DIARY
of 2/10 Scott of ? KLR
INTELLIGENCE SUMMARY

Army Form C. 2118

(Erase heading not required.)

Place	Date	Hour	Summary of Events and Information	Remarks and references to Appendices
TRENCHES BOISGRENIER SECTOR FLAMENGRIE SS	May 19		Our operations - Artillery. Quiet. L.G's - Claim to have inflicted casualties on working party in INCOMPLETE TR: Aircraft. Our planes brought down in flames 2 hostile observation balloon opposite ARMENTIERES at 7.30 p.m. Enemy's Operations - Artillery Quiet T.M. Three minenwerfers have been active recently operating from approximately the following positions. I 21.c.94.14, I 27.a 01.09 & I 32 a 90.05. on COLLEGE GR: KIWI Av & WATER Fm localities respectively. Considerable minor movement observed in rear of Enemy's line. General. One of our NCO's was wounded by a splinter from a bayonet, broken by a rifle bullet. The bayonet was being carried by one of the trench patrol whilst going round the trenches.	Q.82
	May 20		Our operations Artillery Quiet M.T.M. - Fired on Enemy wire in front of INCONSISTENT TR: with good results. - Our L.T.M. created a diversion by firing on INCREASE TR: Retaliation negligible. Repairs - Usual routine work continued nightly on parapet and wire -	Q.87

WAR DIARY
6/2/10 Scottish/6/KLR
INTELLIGENCE SUMMARY

Army Form C. 2118

(Erase heading not required.)

Instructions regarding War Diaries and Intelligence Summaries are contained in F. S. Regs., Part II. and the Staff Manual respectively. Title Pages will be prepared in manuscript.

Place	Date	Hour	Summary of Events and Information	Remarks and references to Appendices
TRENCHES BOIS GRENIER SECTOR FLEURBAIX SS	May 20		Enemies Operations:- Artillery. Quiet.- T.Ms - a few minenwerfers continue to be used on us at intervals M.G. - Fairly active during the night also fixed rifle firing - movement - inclusive of trolleys use and hauled bench in rear of enemies lines at night.	6/Sp
	21		Our operations Artillery - Quiet but fired in retaliation and supported on T.M. shoot. TM - Fired on wire in front of INCONSISTENT - retaliation fairly heavy LTM - Supported medium by firing on INCREASE TR. Maintenance - New wire erected in 3 places along our front Enemies Operations Artillery. Quiet - retaliation mainly confined to minnies from fire and rifle grenades fired which a considerable number trench were Sent over in reply to our TM shoot. a direct hit blocking SAFETY ALLEY Options. Noises of large working parties heard at night in enemy trenches	9/Sp
	22		Our operations Artillery - active at intervals during the day especially during the Afternoon in retaliation to enemy T.M.s. M.T.M. fired on our left flank, provoking fairly heavy retaliation on our sector	8/Sp

1875 Wt. W593/826 1,000,000 4/15 J.B.C. & A. A.D.S.S./Forms/C. 2118.

WAR DIARY
2/10 Scottish [?] 2/10 KLR
INTELLIGENCE SUMMARY

Army Form C. 2118

Instructions regarding War Diaries and Intelligence Summaries are contained in F.S. Regs., Part II. and the Staff Manual respectively. Title Pages will be prepared in manuscript.

(Erase heading not required.)

Place	Date	Hour	Summary of Events and Information	Remarks and references to Appendices
TRENCHES BOIS GRENIER SECTOR FLAMENGRIE SS	May 22 (contd)		**Our Operations (contd)** LTM assisted in above shoot firing on INCREASE TR. and in retaliation to Pineapples. Repairs, usual routine repairs and wiring carried out. **Enemy operations** Artillery - Fairly active throughout the day, mostly with heavies on rear cuts of WHITE CITY, & LEICESTER SQ. T.M. active during day - especially in COLLEGE GREEN LOCALITY, where several bays completely demolished by MINNIES.	
"	"		The 2/9 KLR relieved the 2/10 KLR (less A.Co of 2/10 KLR remaining in the Subsidiary Line). Relief completed without incident, and the 2/10 KLR	
STREAKY BACON & LA ROLANDERIE FMS.	May 23		Less A Co marched to usual billets in STREAKY BACON & LA ROLANDERIE FMS. 2 Lt P St J Rathbone reported for duty, transposed to B Coy. Owing to baths at ERQUING HEM having been put out of action, thorough smell fine - the baths at SAILLY were utilized instead.	
NEAR ERQUINGHEM	"	24 25	Usual training and night working parties in front line. At 11.5 pm on the night of the 25 ellry, 180 gas projectors were fired by us simultaneously on enemy front trench lines at INCONSISTENT (I.32.a.) The gas appeared to diffuse satisfactorily and rolled rearward along the enemy front trench lines. Only increased M.G. activity + a large number of S.O.S	

WAR DIARY
INTELLIGENCE SUMMARY

Of 2/10 Scottish or 10 KLR

Army Form C. 2118

Place	Date	Hour	Summary of Events and Information	Remarks and references to Appendices
STREAKY BACON & LA ROLANDERIE FMS	May 26		At about 1.30 am a fighting patrol consisting of 2 Officers 2 Sergeants and 36 OR left our trenches at I.32.a.04.75 – and moved across NML with a view to entering the enemy trench at I.32.a.50.35 to secure an identification and inflict losses on the enemy. The fighting patrol only reached to about 50 yds from the enemies wire, when they were fired on by 3 M.Gs. one on their R and two on their L of the gap in the enemies wire at I.32.a.50.35. which had previously been cut – The enemy sent up numerous verey lights and also turned on a portable search light, which appeared to be worked from his front line on the patrol. The patrol suffered in consequence comparatively severely losing two men killed 9 wounded (one gunshot since died) and 2 Lt Mackinnell wounded. 2nd Lt Fairclough (who went in the enemy trench) gave the order to withdraw, after the surprise was obviously useless, this was successfully accomplished, all the dead & wounded being brought back from trenches, there are no missing. Usual training and rifle working parties carried out. B Coy 2/10 KLR relieved A Coy 2/10 KLR in subsidiary line, the latter returned to STREAKY BACON FARM BILLETS.	

Army Form C. 2118

WAR DIARY
INTELLIGENCE SUMMARY
(Erase heading not required.)

Instructions regarding War Diaries and Intelligence Summaries are contained in F.S. Regs, Part II. and the Staff Manual respectively. Title Pages will be prepared in manuscript.

Place	Date	Hour	Summary of Events and Information	Remarks and references to Appendices
STREAKY BACON & LA ROLANDERIE FMS	May 27		Whit Sunday - Usual services and working party at night in front line -	
	28		Whit Monday. Usual training in morning - Batn Sports in afternoon in meadow near River Lys at ERQUINGHEM were a great success -	
	28		Pt/Col. E W RODDY proceeded to England on 10 days leave - Major W H MAXWELL taking command 2/Lt R Wallace 2/7 Bn S yr min reported for duty - were posted to B & 6 Coys respectively	
	29		Usual training and night watering parties -	
	30		Battalion parade near ERQUINGHEM CHURCH	
IN TRENCHES BOIS GRENIER SECTOR PLOEGSTEERT	31		Battalion relieved 1st K.R.R. in trenches, relief completed without incident at 11.25 pm. C Coy on left, D Co in centre, A Co on Right & B Coy in Subs Line 1 Coy of 2/19 KLR remained in subsidiary line	
SS	31		Our operations Artillery - very quiet Maintenance - General Routine work carried on Enemy operations Artillery Generally very quiet General - Quiet But knows	
	May 1		Total Battalion strength - 48 officers 1001 O.R.s	
	" 31		" " 52 officers 990 O.R.s	

1875 Wt. W593/826 1,000,000 4/15 J.B.C. & A. A.D.S.S./Form/C. 2118.

War Diary
of
9/10th (Scottish) Battn The King's (Liverpool Regiment)

Period
1st June 1917 to 30th June 1917

In the Field
1·7·1917

Instructions regarding War Diaries and Intelligence Summaries are contained in F.S. Regs., Part II. and the Staff Manual respectively. Title Pages will be prepared in manuscript.

WAR DIARY of 2/10TH (SCOTTISH) BN. KING'S LIVERPOOL REGIMENT

INTELLIGENCE SUMMARY

(Erase heading not required.)

Army Form C. 2118

Place	Date	Hour	Summary of Events and Information	Remarks and references to Appendices
BOIS GRENIER FLAMANGERIE SUBSECTOR Map Reference 36 N.W. 4 7A	1/6/17		Our 18 pounder fired about 50 rounds on enemy trenches at INCOMPLETE otherwise artillery normal from this subsector. Our T.M. fired on enemy trench (?) knocking out a Snyper Post, a good deal of retaliation resulted. Enemy active with "Pineapples" on night of return. Enemy Aeroplane flew low over N.M.L. & fired at men in trench at 12.03. No damage done & plane was driven off. Our Snypers claimed one hit. Lt Jowett & six O.R. attempted to enter enemy trenches during night but were seen & driven off by rifle & M.G. fire. Casualties Nil.	Pt.
	2/6/17		Quiet day. Enemy used "Pineapples" at intervals. Our T.M. fired with good results, our shell exploding on an ammunition dump. Usual patrolling carried out during night. No enemy met. Casualties 5 wounded. 2 of which returned to duty.	Pt.
	3/6/17		Very quiet day. Enemy dropped five "Minnies" on COLLEGE GREEN locality damaging several fire bays. Snipers claimed a hit on enemy snyper. Patrolling much hindered by bright moon light. Casualties N.I.L.	Pt.
	4/6/17		Our artillery active during day. Enemy artillery showed increased activity mostly on back areas. ERQUINGHEM – RUE MARLE & ARMENTIERES being shelled. Enemy also appeared to register on our front line & N.M.L. at INCOME TRENCH from shells being fired. Bright moon again interfered with patrolling. Casualties One wounded slightly.	Pt.
	5/6/17		Our artillery active all day, infact very during afternoon. Enemy artillery fairly active on back areas. Enemy showed considerable activity with his T.M. Our snypers claimed one hit on a man an INCREASE 2 Lieut. J DARROCH was wounded in the foot during the afternoon otherwise no casualties	Pt.

WAR DIARY OF 2/10TH (SCOTTISH) BN. KING'S LIVERPOOL REGIMENT

INTELLIGENCE SUMMARY

Army Form C. 2118

Instructions regarding War Diaries and Intelligence Summaries are contained in F.S. Regs., Part II. and the Staff Manual respectively. Title Pages will be prepared in manuscript.

(Erase heading not required.)

Place	Date	Hour	Summary of Events and Information	Remarks and references to Appendices
BOIS GRENIER	6/6/17		Our artillery + T M's carried out a combined shoot during the afternoon on the enemy trenches opposite the ROE DU BOIS subsector. The enemy replied with heavy retaliation S.O.S. & 'Minnies'. The left of our subsector coming in for a share of this. Quiet day otherwise. Cornwallis Fore wounded.	P.t.
FLAMANGERIE SUBSECTOR	7/6/17		Enemy artillery quiet during day on subsector. He appeared to register again on his front line at Treverez exactly from INCOME Farm shells being fired. (Operations at MESSINES commenced 3-10 AM Mine explosions distinctly felt + Artillery Bombardment seen + heard in our lines	P.t.
Map Reference 36 N W 4 7 A		9.30 pm 11.50 pm	The 2/9th K.L.R. commenced to relieve the Scottish in the subsector Relief reported complete. During the whole night the enemy continuously shelled the Cross roads & cross roads immediately in the vicinity of Battalion Headquarters at H.17 d.4.3. The farm at H.17 d.4.3 was used as Battalion Headquarters for the first time by the Scottish	
FARM at H.17 d.4.3 nr ROLANDERIE & LATEEM FARM.	8/6/17		Battalion in rest billets, day devoted to bath + cleaning equipment, arms etc. C.O. returned from leave in England.	P.t.
	9/6/17		Battalion in Rest Billets. Training + Head Working Parties etc.	N.t.M.
	10/6/17		"	N.t.M.
	11/6/17		"	M.t.M.
	12/6/17		" Gun Position at GRIS POT badly shelled during the evening. Our casualties 2, on road behind.	W.t.M.
	13/6/17		Transport inspected by O.C. Div Train	B.t.M.
	14/6/17		MAJOR W.H.MAXWELL proceeded on 10 days leave to ENGLAND A.2nd left in subsidiary mine.	W.M.W.

2/4 K.L.R. relieved in trenches by 12th Portuguese Regt.

WAR DIARY of the 2/10th (SCOTTISH) KING'S (LIVERPOOL) Regt Army Form C. 2118

INTELLIGENCE SUMMARY

Instructions regarding War Diaries and Intelligence Summaries are contained in F.S. Regs., Part II. and the Staff Manual respectively. Title Pages will be prepared in manuscript.

(Erase heading not required.)

Place	Date	Hour	Summary of Events and Information	Remarks and references to Appendices
FARM at H.17.d.4.3	15/6/17		(B Coy relieved A Coy in Subsidiary Line)	
CANTEEN FARM La Rolanderie	16/6/17		Battalion in Rest Billets. Usual Training & Working Parties	WNm/
MAP REFERENCE 36 N.W.4	17/6/17			
	18/6/17			
	19/6/17		Battalion relieved in Brigade Reserve by 2/4th Battn. K.L.R. & moved at 8 pm to Rest Billets in Erquinghem. B Coy relieved in Subsidiary Line by Company 1/9 KLR	
	20/6/17			
ERQUINGHEM	21/6/17			WNm/
	22/6/17			
	23/6/17		Battalion in Rest Billets. Usual Training & Working Parties	
	24/6/17			
	25/6/17			
	26/6/17		MAJOR W.H. MAXWELL returned from leave in England.	
	27/6/17		During early hours of the morning Bosch attempted a raid close to BRIDOUX SALIENT. There & Working Parties of C & D were moving Gaps & cutting wire. A heavy barrage was put down resulting in 10 casualties. Capt Alan Cookson Jenny killed, also Sergt A. Muir (B Coy.) & Pte F. Johns D Coy. 2d Lieut E.H. Hollins and 2d Lieut W. Sargeant (Samson Alderhausen) Pte A. Jones (B Coy) B. Myherico, L/Cpl Blagg D & S. Hayside & Trigg L/Cpl L. AM. Battalion relieved 9th PORTUGESE Regt. in FLAMANGERIE Subsector. Relief Complete 1 am (BOIS GRENIER)	WNm/

WAR DIARY
of the 2/10 (SCOTTISH) Kings (LIVERPOOL) Regt
or INTELLIGENCE SUMMARY

Army Form C. 2118

Place	Date	Hour	Summary of Events and Information	Remarks and references to Appendices
BOIS GRENIER FLAMANGERIE SUB SECTOR Map Reference 36 NW H.4 7A	28/6/17		Our Artillery active during day. About 30 Rounds HOWITZER fire on new (Enemy) Front to left of I.26.5.at.130. H + M.T.M's fired 68 rounds on Enemy's wire I.26.6-65.00. from 4.30-6.30 pm Short Satisfactory. Enemy wire obviously demolished. Enemy retaliated with Salvos of Whiz bangs, Pine Apples, Light & heavy "Minnies" batten effectively dealt with by 4.5 How. Battery. L.T.M's. fired on INCLEMENT SUPPORT & INCOME TRENCH in retaliation to Minnies. Enemy Artillery fairly active on front line during the day with Whiz bangs. T.M's Very active during day with "Minnies". Direct hit on R.H.Q College Green with Rumjar [Small Minnie]	[initials]
"	29/6/17		Our Artillery. Two Batteries engaged in wire Cutting in INDEX TRENCH in Connection with RAID between 10 AM and 12.30 pm. An Intense Barrage opened at 3.5 pm in accordance with operation orders for RAID. M.T.M's. Three Batteries engaged on wire Cutting in INDEX TRENCH in Connection with RAID Between 5.30 + 8.15 A.M. All Batteries opened at ZERO hour in accordance with operation orders. 3.L.T.M's Co-operated in RAID. M+L Guns. Cooperated in Raid, also active against Enemy Planes. Special Report of the Raid by "C" Coy at 3.5 pm is attached Separately. CASUALTIES to above RAID KILLED 2 OR Missing (since killed) 2 OR Missing (since wounded) 3 OR Missing 2 OR Wounded 2 OR 1.14. 8. 48. Enemy Observation. During Day Enemy attention was mainly Concerned with own RAID Throughout the Enemy Severely Shelled TOCKIS TOY and at least 50% of his Shells in that Area are reported to have been "DUDS" Considerable damage done to our Front + Subsurface lines in places The fired in retaliation to our wire Cutting operation + Caused Considerable damage to our front line EAST of BRIDOUX SALIENT during Raid but Shelly appeared to tell well to his left it our Raiding Party N.G. was heavily engaged our Northern flank braving Enemy wires during Raid.	[initials]

WAR DIARY
or of the 2/10" (SCOTTISH) KINGS (LIVERPOOL) Reg.
INTELLIGENCE SUMMARY
(Erase heading not required.)

Army Form C. 2118

Instructions regarding War Diaries and Intelligence Summaries are contained in F.S. Regs., Part II. and the Staff Manual respectively. Title Pages will be prepared in manuscript.

Place	Date	Hour	Summary of Events and Information	Remarks and references to Appendices
BOIS GRENIER FLAMANGERIE Sub-Sector MAP Reference 36. N.W.4 M.A.	30/10/17		Our trenches received shelling during day by 18 Pounders, 60 Pounders & Minnenwerfers. Patrols out during night searching M.N.E opposite BRIDOUX SALIENT. Enemy trenches Quiet throughout the day. Little attempt made by Enemy to effect repairs to his trenches more in INDEX TRENCH. Weather Steady Rain all day.	M.M.N

DICKY'S DASH

172ND INFANTRY BRIGADE
57th DIVISION

REPORT OF MINOR OPERATION CARRIED OUT IN THE BOIS GRENIER SECTION

on the day of 29th June 1917

by the 2/10th (Scottish) Battalion The King's (Liverpool Regiment)
Lieut:Colonel E.L.RODDY Commanding.

***

STRENGTH OF PARTY.	161 of "C" Company commanded by Captain A.P.Dickinson, plus one Platoon of "A" Company remaining in our Lines as a Reserve.
POINT OF EXIT.	The BOW of the BRIDOUX SALIENT.
POINT OF ENTRY.	Between I.31.d.03.25 and I.31.c.90.10.
TIME.	3-5.p.m.
OBJECT.	To destroy as many of the enemy as possible and to bring back identifications and booty.
NARRATIVE.	See attached.

NARRATIVE OF A RAID ON THE ENEMY'S TRENCHES SOUTH OF BOIS GRENIER OPPOSITE THE BRIDOUX SALIENT ON THE AFTERNOON OF THE 29th JUNE 1917, BY "C" COMPANY OF THE 2/10th (SCOTTISH) BATTALION KING'S L-POOL REG, BEING KNOWN AS "DICKY'S DASH".

PREPARATION. On the night before the Raid our own wire was cut. At dawn on "Z" day our Trench Mortars cut enemy's wire until 8.0 a.m., at which hour the Brigade Intelligence Officer reported that he was not quite satisfied. Thereupon, as previously arranged, 18 pounders carried on the wire cutting until the Intelligence Officer reported that all was satisfactory.

ASSEMBLY. ZERO hour was fixed for 3.5 p.m. The men had a meal at 11.0 a.m. with a "tot" of rum, and were equipped and ready to move off at noon, when watches were finally synchronized.
Half the raiding party then proceeded via HUDSON BAY AVENUE and the other half by SHAFTESBURY & TRAMWAY AVENUES, in sections of 200 yards interval.
Both parties reached the Salient at opposite ends and crawled into their assembly positions, reaching same half an hour before ZERO according to orders.

1st PHASE. ZERO to ZERO plus 2.
Our 18 pounders opened on the enemy's Front Line with intense fire at the portion to be entered. Machines of the Corps squadron R.F.C. dropping bombs on the flanks of the raid area. Howitzers opened on selected spots, on which they fired during whole operation. An observer in an O.P. states that the men "went across in magnificent style" in two waves. They reached the enemy line without a casualty, no rifle or machine gun fire being opened on them.
Our men got close up to our own barrage waiting for the moment that it lifted at ZERO plus 2, when they simultaneously rushed the trench, finding no difficulty with the wire which was completely obliterated. A few casualties were suffered by a few . of our men who got too close to our own barrage.

2nd PHASE. ZERO plus 2 to ZERO plus 7.
Barrage lifted to enemy support line. The right party met with little opposition: a block on the right front trench was formed immediately.
The right communication trench party whose objective was the enemy support line failed to find the right hand C.T. down which they were to work, as it was obliterated. This party met with a little opposition which was immediately dealt with. Many enemy dead and wounded were lying about in their locality. The Lewis Gun with this party got very quickly into a good position on the parados, from which they immediately found a target of a body of the enemy in the open, who had been ejected from some shell holes by our bombers. This gun then knocked out a hostile M.G. which had been mounted on the Support Line described as being half right.
The left party entered the trench but found considerable resistance especially behind the NOSE, when a bombing fight ensued in which all the enemy were killed. A Lewis Gun here came into action and silenced a hostile party on the left flank.
Hereabouts a deep dugout was found with a steel door into which a "P" bomb was thrown just as the door was about to be closed upon which many Germans rushed

out ten or twelve being killed as they emerged. Two prisoners were taken here and on refusing to get over the parapet were killed.

This dugout had two entrances, out of the second entrance another party of Germans emerged who ran down the left Communication trench, down which a party of our men had already gone, half being outside and half inside the trench.

All ranks of the left party state that on entering the trench they found a great many enemy dead laying about, as the result of our artillery fire.

Corporal Lester, in Lt: Jowett's parapet party (Lt: Jowett being killed in the 1st Phase) states -
" I went through the third gap in the Bosche wire from the right; 6 Germans looked over the enemy front line parapet and were blown up by a shell. I saw a lot of dead Bosches in a concrete dugout; two prisoners were sent back to me from the left but before reaching me suddenly dashed behind the traverse on to the tramline behind. I at once pursued and succeeded in shooting the rear man who wore a white band round his cap. The first man was dealt with by some of our people who were on the tramline."

Lt: Jowett just before he was killed exchanged shots with a German officer with his revolver and killed him, Lt: Jowett being then killed by two bombs.

The Centre Party detailed for the enemy front line rushed the trench immediately the barrage lifted, a general bombing fight ensued, all Germans found in the trench were bayonetted, those remaining in dugouts were ejected by "P" bombs and killed as they emerged.

3rd PHASE.
ZERO plus 7 to ZERO plus 30

The left communication trench party proceeded half over land and half down the trench according to orders.
The bombing party formed a block at the entrance to INDEX DRIVE, and the remainder proceeded up the Support Line where considerable resistance was encountered.
2nd Lt: Blencowe in charge of this party was last seen proceeding over land along the outside of the Support Trench where an officer had been seen directing the German operations from the parapet until one of our men shot him. Sergeant Kelly who was with the support of this party states that he saw a German very cooly mounting an automatic rifle in the support line; the Sergt fired and killed the man. The right communication trench party were unable to carry out their full programme of the 3rd Phase owing to the destruction of the trench.

WITHDRAW.
From ZERO plus 30.

The withdrawal signal was given by the blowing of whistles and bugles both in our own lines and the enemy's. The withdrawal was carried out according to programme except that a certain number of our men rushed back to our own lines and there suffered a considerable number of casualties from the hostile barrage.
Ditches had been previously reconnoitred on both flanks of the BRIDOUX SALIENT in NO MAN'S LAND, into which our men had been told to lay up until things got quiet or darkness came on. The position of these ditches had been carefully shown to the whole company by the O.C. Raid on the blackboard during lectures on the raid.
Those men who obeyed these orders returned safely after dark.

PRISONERS.

In addition to the four prisoners previously mentioned who were killed whilst endeavoring to escape, three more were sent over the parapet towards our lines; two of these were killed in the enemy barrage in NO MAN'S LAND and the third who took cover in a shellhole was shot by our men during the withdrawal.

CO-OPERATION WITH ROYAL FLYING CORPS.	The utmost assistance was rendered by the co-operation of the Corps Squadron R.F.C., who greatly assisted the entry and withdrawal by dropping bombs on the flanks of the raided area, firing with their Machine Guns on a large party of the enemy who rushed back from their support line across the open just as our raiding party entered the front line, and also by firing into the enemy trenches.
OUR CASUALTIES.	Most of the casualties suffered by our men were inflicted by bombs while in the enemy's line and by "Minnies" and shell fire in our front line after the withdrawal. The whole of the 6 definitely known to be killed were killed by a "Minnie" in our front line.
ENEMY'S CASUALTIES.	At a conservative estimate the number of dead seen in German trenches by our men ranges from 60 to 70, not including the casualties inflicted by the flying corps and our artillery fire beyond the raided area.
ENEMY'S MORAL.	From all accounts the enemy moral is good; he mounted Machine Guns on his parapets in the middle of our barrage and exposed himself with coolness whilst throwing bombs and sniping.
OUR MACHINE GUNS.	During the whole of the operation a box barrage was maintained round the raiding party. Guns were also firing on the flanks of the points of entry.
LEWIS GUNS.	During the raid the Lewis Guns that were sent forward knocked out several of the enemy machine guns at close range, and also dealt with parties of the enemy in the open. Fire from our rear was kept on the enemy's observation posts in trees.
TRENCH MORTAR BATTERIES.	MEDIUM. Cut the enemy's wire from dawn until 8.0 a.m. on "Z" day under heavy retaliation. A diversion was also formed 800 yards away on the left of the attack during the operation. LIGHT. 200 shells were dropped from ZERO to ZERO plus 2, on the BRIDOUX FORT, and afterwards formed a protective barrage on the enemy's front line on the flanks of the attack at points which could not be dealt with by our artillery. The enemy's rifle and machine gun fire was kept down during the withdrawal. In all 1210 rounds were fired.
ARTILLERY.	OURS. Most accurate and effective; the enemy's wire was cut by 18-pounders using the 106 fuze at points which had not been sufficiently dealt with by the Medium Trench Mortars. They completed the work very satisfactory. ENEMY'S. A light barrage came down on our front line at ZERO plus 2. This was much intensified at ZERO plus 15 and continued to ZERO plus 60 on our front, support & communication trenches. It was noticed that the enemy barraged his own front line on the right flank of the attack including part of the right of the objective. At ZERO plus 20 onwards N.M.L. was barraged slightly.
SIGNALS.	Telephone communication from our Front Line to advanced Bn H.Q. was maintained until 10 minutes after the withdrawal. Visual signalling continued all through satisfactorily. Communication forward from O.C. Raid to O.C. Assault was not satisfactory owing to casualties incurred by the party.

Brig. General.
Commanding 172nd Infantry Bde.

WAR DIARY or INTELLIGENCE SUMMARY

Army Form C. 2118

of the 1/10th (SCOTTISH) KING'S (Liverpool) Regt

Vol 6

Place	Date	Hour	Summary of Events and Information	Remarks and references to Appendices
BOIS CARRÉ	1/7/19		Patrols out during night searching NNE in front of BRIDOUX SALIENT	
FERMANDERIE Sub Sector			Our Operations. Artillery quiet on this Subsector. H&T M2 did not fire. M.Guns fired on Haikle Aircraft. Aircraft active. General Quiet behind Visibility fair only.	WNM
Right Section & R.M.E.			Enemy Operations. Artillery active in neighbourhood of BURNT FARM. Aeroplanes Reconnoitring along his own front line heavily fired on by our M.G's. General Very Quiet. Enemy trench M.G. along no man's line troubled us during the night.	
	2/7/19		Our Operations. Patrols out in front of BRIDOUX SALIENT all night searching for missing, wounded or dead men heartily. Our Artillery Quiet. Attention continues to be given to Enemy's known areas. Wire Parapet in front of Bridoux Salient. Aircraft. Very active all day. General Visibility good, Quiet [during?]	WNM
			Enemy Operations. Artillery quiet all day. TM's active at intervals. Aircraft. Very active This evening during the evening, a number of Enemy planes crossed our lines between 10 to 11 pm. General. Quiet. Enemy evidently devoting his attention to work in his trenches.	
	3/7/19		Our Operations. Patrols. Bright Moonlight rendered Patrolling difficult. Artillery active during evening against Enemy's front line subjects Ultimo area and shelled H & M.T.M. fire from the subsector during the day. M.Gs. fired on Enemy Aircraft during day. Wire Bright moonlight prevented much wiring being carried out in front of our trenches. Aircraft. Active during day & night. General Visibility had improved. Other situation quiet.	
			Enemy Operations. Artillery Active at intervals. One HTM. shown SHROPNEL & HEMM, in position at CHARING CROSS & CHAPTER ROW. At dawn ½ to 2 short bursts 10am. Very light sent up in enemy steadily ... followed by 3 Shown of Green Lights. Aircraft. Active. General Enemy must quiet. Seems to be evading sniping behind his lines.	WNM

WAR DIARY of 2/10 (SCOTTISH) KING'S (LIVERPOOL) Regt.

INTELLIGENCE SUMMARY

Place	Date	Hour	Summary of Events and Information	Remarks and references to Appendices
BOIS GRENIER	3/7/17		**Our Operations** Patrols Nil. Artillery Active on Enemy front line, support, & back areas. MTMs fired 60 Rounds into trenches in Index & to right of Bridoux Rd. Went & bombed much damaged Retaliation heavy but from Minnies & H.E's. 2 coils Wire. No wire parties in front and Aircraft Normal Patrolling. General Visibility fair. Rations, Rum, but Quiet infrom at Night. **Enemy Operations** Artillery Active. College Green heavily under. Burnt Farm Tramway Av Trench Joy & Leicester Square all received attention. 60 Minnies fell in College Green Kiwi & Leicester. Half of those went on wire in N.K. Pineapples front along armoured Support line, that is the 2nd day the locality has received special attention from Minnies. Range of TMs has been increased or mortars have moved as Aircraft Enemy Shoots over own lines between N & 11 from.	Nil
	4/7/17		**Our Operations** Patrols Nil. Artillery Active at intervals during the day. Six Citizens attended effective retaliation to active Minnie "Rumjars". Quiet during night. MTMs fired in Enemy's wire under trench mat to right of Bridoux Road with good effect. General Visibility for improvised lakes. Generally Quiet. **Enemy Operations** Artillery active at intervals. Burnt Farm & Bois Grenier Shelled S.W. Minnies on Safety Alley. At 7AM the Enemy commenced a steady bombardment of machines between Park Row & Stanway Av with "Minnies" "Rum-jars" and "Pineapples". The Pineapples reaching well over Support line (Reuter Range Than usual) In Kiwi & Kin Sector. 42 Minnies + Rumjars were counted and at least 100 Pineapples. Our Artillery retaliated effectively & fire ceased at 7:45 AM. General Quiet period. Enemy Shell Shorts 87M of Nervousness, harassing Hstrny M.Guns along his own line.	Nil
	6/7/17		**Our Operations** Patrols Nil. Artillery Ammun firm 18 pdrs fired on Enemy Front line System. MTMs fired on Targets in Index Trench & Right of Bridoux Rd. 4-5 pm. Aircraft active all day over Enemy's lines. General Visibility Good. Quiet during day. **Enemy Operations** Artillery active during day. Bois Grenier Shelled during Evening. T.Ms 12 Minnies on Park Row Trench Joy & Kiwi Av. The following A.W.O. and Military Medal in Connection with Enemy Raid ref - Lieut AH Lester, Ptes CH GAYLE & S RITCHINGS, J STONE & C DAVIS. Pte N GLANZON & Cpl E PEAVER.	Nil

1875 Wt. W593/826 1,000,000 4/15 J.B.C. & A. A.D.S.S./Forms/C. 2118.

WAR DIARY or INTELLIGENCE SUMMARY

1/8th 2/10 (SCOTTISH) KINGS (Liverpool) Regt

Army Form C. 2118

(Erase heading not required.)

Instructions regarding War Diaries and Intelligence Summaries are contained in F.S. Regs., Part II. and the Staff Manual respectively. Title Pages will be prepared in manuscript.

Place	Date	Hour	Summary of Events and Information	Remarks and references to Appendices
Bois GRENIER FLEURBAIX Sub Sector Map Reference 36 NW 4 + 36A	Night of 6/7 Sept 1917		Extracts from Special Report on Hostile Barrage and Expected Raid on Rue du Bois Sub-Sector. Diversion. About 9.45 pm Enemy opened a Barrage or Barrages on Fleurbaix Sub-Sector, mostly very heavy "Minnie" fire at 10 pm enemy opened our intense Barrage on T.21.5 + T.21.u. from Front Support line, creeping back to Second Support line. The Box Barrage was put on Rue du Bois S.T. within Sturt trench Queen Street Wine Street & Front line of Rue du Bois Sub Sector. The Minnie Barrage was of the utmost intensity. Air bursts & ground bursts, being most accurate and completely demolishing certain localities especially junction of C.T.'s, Kiwi, Tramway Av, Shaftesbury Av, Support line from Kiwi to College Green. College Green locality, Teddy-Burrow + Mackenzie Hospital all suffered considerably. Maori Minnies also fell in Locre Joy + Neighbourhood. E.T.'s were principally dealt with by Air Burst Minnies + H.E Shrapnel (time fuse). Our enemy aeroplanes were over our lines during the whole of the operation + dropped White Red Lights. At 10.15 pm our Artillery opened fire on enemy Front & Support Lines. The Enemy Barrage had lifted from our front line when this happened. At 10.20 pm on F.T. No's + No Bois Sub-Sector as previously arranged in area between Cowgate & Wine Av (Rue du Bois Sub-Sector) as previously arranged. At about 10.50 pm Enemy Barrage began to slacken when previously arranged parties worked up all S.T's + an Enemy Barrage permitted (now go forward, Scouted Front line found in between two Support line victorious later. A patrol of 2 officers & 20 O.R's from H.Q. & Reinf Regt thoroughly searched N.M.L within 30 yds of German wire. No trace whatever was found of the Enemy in N.M.L run could any traces be found from his front line. None of the enemy entered our trench except a small party who entered in Rue de Bois Sub Sect which a few German stick grenades were thrown. In the morning (2 men and 1 Hun with gun kills Lee). The Barrage on this Sub-Sector lasted full midnight & occasional Minnies Overswar up till 12.30 am.	
			Our Casualties: Killed 2 (Pte Head Roberts Spiller) Died of Wounds 2 (Pte Stanley Moore) Wounded 20 Total 24. Wounded Cpl F.A. 1412 Drought (1147) Taylor Lord Birdies Mc Bennison Between Dunn Bay-Sgt Pugsley Carr Cunnells Duffy Barrows Herron Taylor Snyman Walker Hatchett Stephens (Attwood Jr Taylor Northern Rifle Royal No. 501)	

1875 Wt. W593/826 1,000,000 4/15 J.B.C. & A. A.D.S.S./Forms/C. 2118.

WAR DIARY
or
INTELLIGENCE SUMMARY

Army Form C. 2118

1/Bn 2/10th (SCOTTISH) KING'S (Liverpool) Regt.

(Erase heading not required.)

Instructions regarding War Diaries and Intelligence Summaries are contained in F.S. Regs, Part II. and the Staff Manual respectively. Title Pages will be prepared in manuscript.

Place	Date	Hour	Summary of Events and Information	Remarks and references to Appendices
BOIS GRENIER FLAMANGERIE Sub Sector	7/7/17		Own operations. Patrols. None out owing to moonlight. Artillery. Slight activity during day. 18 Pounders 4.5 How fired in retaliation to Minnie during the evening. Two direct hits on T132.6.25.30. Three new Series running out of Emplacement H.M.T.Ms. fired on Tampers – INDEX Trench to right of BRIDGE Rd. General. Quiet. Period. Visibility fair.	
MAP Reference 36 N.W.4. 7A			Enemy Operations. Quieter than usual. Between 6 & 9 pm TOCKS TOP, SHAFTESBURY AV, TRAMWAY Ave. were shelled & 'Minnies' Active during day. Patrolling over new trench. General. Very quiet period, except during T.M. activity.	
	8/7/17		Own Operations. Patrols None out. Artillery generally quiet during day. M.T.Ms at 5 pm fired on Trench in INDEX TRENCH to right of BRIDGE Road. Aircraft Inactive General Patrolled areas for Enemy Operations. Quiet Artillery. Quiet during night. No M. TMs. TOCKS Top & SAFETY ALLEY received some attention during afternoon. Aircraft Inactive	
	9/7/17		Relieved by 2/4 K.L.R. Relief completed by 11 pm. Quiet day generally.	
FARM at H.M.Q.D.			Billets. Baths. Kit Inspection etc.	
LA ROSSIGNERIE FARM & ERQUINGHEM	10/7/17			
	11/7/17		→ Divisional Commander (Maj General BARNES) presented Military Medal Ribbon to Cpl. LEETCH. Pte RITCHINGS & Sergt WELBON & Pte C. SAMMONS Co. Gunnery Distinguished Conduct Medal.	
	12/7/17		Pte GAYLE Dis. Landon. Working parties &c.	
	13/7/17		13.7.17. 2nd Lieuts. L.B. ASTLEY & 2/C McKIBBIN reported from 3rd Line. Posted to D & B Companies.	
	14/7/17			
	15/7/17			

WAR DIARY
of the 2/10 (Scottish) KINGS (Liverpool) Regt
INTELLIGENCE SUMMARY

Army Form C. 2118

Instructions regarding War Diaries and Intelligence Summaries are contained in F.S. Regs, Part II. and the Staff Manual respectively. Title Pages will be prepared in manuscript.

(Erase heading not required.)

Place	Date	Hour	Summary of Events and Information	Remarks and references to Appendices
FARM at the HINTWH LA RULANDERIE FARM a/c	17/7/17		Billets. Battalion Parade in morning. Battn. moved in evening to Billets in RUE MARLE. (Hqrs at CROWN PRINCE HOUSE) & relieved 2/5th Battn. South Lancashire Regt. in Brigade Reserve (Left Sub-Sector).	WNW
RUE MARLE.	18/7/17		Battalion relieved 2/4th South Lancashire Regt in RUE DU BOIS Sub-Sector. Relief completed by 11 P.M. No 1 Coy, 29th Portuguese Battn. in the line.	WNW
BOIS GRENIER RUE DU BOIS Sub Sector Map Reference 36 NW U 7A	19/7/17		Our Artillery : Artillery Retaliation on Enemy Supports. Income Inclement Incision & Incident Searching etc. Incline Av. INCONSEAU ALLEY INCLINE Av. Harassing fire on PRENESQUES. PARADISE Rd etc. LTMB fired 10 Rounds on GERMAN HOUSE. 15 in INCLINE TRENCH &c. General. Very quiet period. Enemy Operations Artillery — a Minute 10.5cm on Subsid. line WINE Av. to WELLINGTON. 7.7cm on LEITH WALK CHARD'S FARM. Random from BIEZ. Supports AVONDALE & WINE TNB Minnies active on COWGATE & CHARD'S FARM. Air Enft. Enemy planes active in evening. General Report. Quiet period. Gas. (250 Cylinders) was projected successfully at 11.30pm via 10 INCISION & INCIDENT System of Supports & ETE reverse Road in WEZ MACQUART. No Special action noted on Enemy's part. No 1 Coy 29th Portuguese Battn left the line. 2nd Lieut WE WHITTON reported from 3rd line & reported to C. Coy.	WNW
	20/7/17		Our Operations. Patrols fighting Patrol lay out in N.M.L. N/W of RUE DU BOIS Salient till 2 AM. All Quiet. Artillery Active Cooperating with T.M. Shoots on WIRE M.T.M.'s fired on WIRE INCLEMENT TRENCH Junction of INCLUDE & INCIDENT LANE, Aircraft Active Patrolling. Sun-down lit Retaliation morale, LTM's Lives in Considerable Artillery activity. General — A period of Considerable Artillery activity. Enemy Operations Artillery Active in retaliation to our TM Shoots during day, & particularly Troublesome at Wire. Between 11pm & 1.30am a Continuous Stream of Gas Shells estimated at 30 per minute (mixed with HE) passed over our lines to their Area including RUE MARLE & CROWN PRINCE HSE Aircraft During our TM shoot an Enemy Plane flew very low over SALLY AVONDALE AVE General "A" and "9". Naval Shell fell at H 6/2 H 5	WNW

1875 Wt. W593/826 1,000,000 4/15 J.B.C. & A. A.D.S.S./Forms/C. 2118.

WAR DIARY
or
INTELLIGENCE SUMMARY
(Erase heading not required.)

Army Form C. 2118

A.16 2/10th (Scottish) Kings (Liverpool) Reg.t

Place	Date	Hour	Summary of Events and Information	Remarks and references to Appendices
BOIS GRENIER Rue du Bois. Sub-Sector. Map Reference 36 NW 1/M T.A.	21/7/19		**Our Operations.** Mouleton Patrols. A pitching patrol of 1 Officer & 11 O.Rs. lay up in N.M.L. on night of R.N.E. Salient. From midnight to 2.30 am no enemy seen or heard of. Enemy. **Artillery.** Fired in retaliation on INDEX, INCIDENT & INCIDENT Subsections. M.TMs. Fired 50 rounds between 7 & 9 p.m. on wire at 126.d.02.27. (INCOMPLETE) & 50 Rounds between 4 & 3.05 a.m. same point - wire destroyed & S.P. cut. Aircraft Very active on enemy special combination quiet patrol. Enemy/Ibeams Continuous shelling of ARMENTIERES. Estimated that between 2000 & 3000 Shells fell — Miscellaneous during 24 hours Generally quiet. Aircraft active during evening.	
	22/7/19		**Our Operations.** Patrols. 1 Officer & 5 O.Rs. lay out in front of our wire at Top of WILLOW AV. from midnight to 2 AM N.M.L. quiet. **Artillery.** Quiet period T.M.B.s Fired on INDEX Subsect. INCLUDE & INCIDENT sub. Subsequently destroying any. Aircraft active patrolling all day. **Enemy Operations.** ARMENTIERES very heavily shelled with shell of all calibres up to 9.2" including portable CROWN PRINCE HOUSE, & Neighbourhood heavily shelled from 2.35 pm to 6 pm. 3000 W.P. & 5.9 shells fired at least 30 Duds were noticed. Many direct hits on the Houses which was wrecked. Casualties, Regt. Were: 4 Men & 6 ORs wounded (gas shells) Between 11 pm & 12.30 AM, Many 300 mm shells were fired on same Target RUE MARIE. Aircraft. Zeppelin seen & heard over the Sub-Sector at Midnight. Capt QRA E RAE reported posted to A. Coy.	
	23/7/19		**Our Operations.** Patrols. 3. Out during night examining Enemy's wire, etc. Enemy quite quiet. Located men in one in front of INCLEMENT. INCLUDE + INCIDENT. Artillery five brought to bear on them. Artillery Quiet period, 4.5 How's destructive shoot. INCLINE AV. A lot of Brick & Concrete houses apparently in the O.T. Aircraft. Very active patrol work. Met with considerable Initiative from A.A. Guns. **Enemy Operations.** Artillery Hostile shelling of ARMENTIERES & RUE MARIE Continued through much less violent than the Sub-Sector. Between 10.30 pm to 11.45 pm. A large number of Gas Shells were fired over the RUE MARIE into King a number of "Casualties", the eyes being much affected Otherwise Artillery was quiet. Aircraft. Active during day. About 2.30 pm. A hostile Squadron of 6 Planes patrolled over our lines & attempted to cross our lines towards ARMENTIERES. One of the Planes were driven down from Low/our lines but our planes continued unmolested. Enemy Planes flying at very large altitudes but Hostile shelling Kept A.A + Machine guns firing. No. 2 Co. 29 D.R. Troops & R.E. Batt. Came into Brine to Bittlinebacks	

1875 Wt. W593/826 1,000,000 4/15 J.B.C. & A. A.D.S.S./Forms/C.2118.

WAR DIARY
or
INTELLIGENCE SUMMARY

of the 2/10 (Scottish) Kings (Liverpool) Regt

Army Form C. 2118

(Erase heading not required.)

Place	Date	Hour	Summary of Events and Information	Remarks and references to Appendices
BOIS GRENIER RUE DU BOIS Sub Sectn Map Reference 36 N.W. 4 T.A.	24/7/17		Our Operations Patrols. 1 Officer + 10 ORs lay up in N.M.L. to right of Rue du Bois Salient. Nothing seen or heard of Enemy. 1 NCO & 3 OR left our lines at 1.16.1. & Located a hostile working Party in INCIDENT. L.G. fire turned on party. Artillery Inactive. Mainly Supporting + Cooperating with H.T.M. Shoots. H.T.M.B. fired 8 rounds between 5+6 p.m. on dug-outs ots 65 yrd North on target. Retaliation heavy. M.T.M.Rs fired 260 rounds on to have in front of INDEX Trench with good results. General Quiet period except for H.T.M. work. Enemy Operations. Artillery Continued Shelling of ARMENTIERES. + RUE MARLE throughout day. Again Major T.M. N/Note absence of fire. only 2 Minnies fired 5:93' + 4.2. & few Shells Predominated. T.M. N/Note absence of fire. only 2 Minnies fired to few rounds on LAWRENCE STREET + LEITH WALK. General Quiet. Artillery limited to back Areas. + retaliation to T.M.s. Enemy Quiet. Artillery limited from Machine. Fired to D.L. Capt. H.T. WHITSON reported from machine. Posted to D.L.	MM
"	25/7/17		Our Operations. Artillery Generally quiet. 4.5 How's fired in Minnie positions. Patrols. Enemy bright 1 Officer + 10 ORs from hand position to right of Rue du Bois Salient. Saw work heard in progress in Enemy lines. M.T.Mb fired 150 rounds on wire + parapet at various points. Good results. Retaliation fairly heavy with Light Minnie. H.E. for shells. Aircraft Quiet except for Wireless H.T. Rhys. Enemy Operations. Quiet period except for retaliation to T.M. Rhys.	MM
"	26/7/17		Our Operations. Patrols. 1 Officer + 4 ORs lay up in neighbourhood of INCIDENT Trench but no Enemy reported in rear. H.T.MS+ run Enemy Support hive in rear. 4.5 H/hrs destructive Artillery 18 Pounders fired on gaps cut H.T.Ms run Enemy Support hive in rear. 4.5 H/hrs destructive Shoot INCISION Av. + retaliation in ENCAMPMENT. Subports. M.T.Ms fired about 150 rounds. M.N.T.b. from Right Sub Secton. Aircraft Active patrolling. General Quiet period Enemy Shelling Artillery very active at times on back area ARMENTIERES, RUE MARLE etc. otherwise a quiet period. Aircraft active at intervals. No 3. Cm 29th PORTUGUESE Battn. Completed turn in line + went out at 9:30p.m. Battn relieved by 2/4th South Lancs Regt Relief Completed by 11:26 p.m. C+D Coys and 1 Platoon of "B" Coy left in line to support 2/4 South Lancs. Hqrs, A. Co. + remainder of "B" marched to Billets at ERQUINGHEM.	MM

WAR DIARY
INTELLIGENCE SUMMARY

Army Form C. 2118

Place	Date	Hour	Summary of Events and Information	Remarks and references to Appendices
ERQUINGHEM	27/7/17		Billets. Baths. Kit Inspections etc.	
	28/7/17		Billets. Inspection of Cookery. 1st Army inspected O.H.C. Stores Workshops etc. addressed Officers, O.Ms, NCOs, Sergeants etc. of the different units of Brigade in afternoon.	
	29/7/17		Billets. Usual Processing Working Parties etc. Between Midnight & 3 AM Enemy intensely bombarded ARMENTIERES & RUE MARLE. Gas Shells in large number were put in between BRICKFIELDS & MUAT FARM, effect felt as far as Brigade Hqrs in Rue Ruffe. Shelling of ARMENTIERES intense. Several extensive fires being caused. *It is estimated that between 6000 & 7000 Gas Shells fell in the Town	
	30/7/17		Billets. Usual Training working Parties. A. Coy released D Coy in S[...]bury line Rue du Bois SubSector ARMENTIERES & RUE MARIE continuously shelled during the day especially in afternoon & evening.	
	31/7/17		Billets. Unusual Training Working Parties, Shelling of ARMENTIERES & RUE MARIE considerably less than previous days past.	

7 X
(8 sheets)

2/10 Liverpool
Vol 7

War Diary
2/10 L'n R.

Army Form C. 2118

WAR DIARY
of the 2/10th (SCOTTISH) KINGS (Liverpool) Regt
INTELLIGENCE SUMMARY
(Erase heading not required.)

Instructions regarding War Diaries and Intelligence Summaries are contained in F.S. Regs, Part II. and the Staff Manual respectively. Title Pages will be prepared in manuscript.

Place	Date	Hour	Summary of Events and Information	Remarks and references to Appendices
ERQUINGHEM	1/8/17		Billets. Usual Training, training parties etc.	
	2/8/17 3/8/17		2/8/17. Major N.H. Maxwell proceeded to AIRE to attend Conference at First Army Artillery School.	WWM
BOIS GRENIER Rue du Bois Sub. Sector. Map Reference 36. N.W.4 7.A.	4/8/17.		Battalion relieved 2/4th South Lancashire Regt in the Rue du Bois Sub Sector. Relief completed 10 p.m. Maxwell.	WWM
	5/8/17		Our operations. Patrols. home out. Artillery very active in Retaliation. Aircraft activity in patrolling & observing during day & again at night. No plane downed on either side. Major W.H. Maxwell returned from Conference & has reported for duty. Enemy Operations Artillery active during day. M. Guns have active than usual. Aircraft fairly active.	10 WWM
	6/8/17		Between 12.5 and 1 AM & between 2 and 2:30 AM. Enemy heavily bombarded our front line & supports with Gas (Mustard) & Shrapnel & HE. chiefly in vicinity of MILLS Rd COWGATE AVONDALE & PARK Rows. (1 OR. wounded). Our operations Patrols 1 NCO & 4 ORs. left CHARD'S FARMS to form listening Post on Enemy wire. No Enemy seen. Patrol reported that Gas Bombardment was effected by T.M.s firing from E.F.L. Artillery fired only in Retaliation. Aircraft active all day. General fairly quiet period. Enemy Operations. ARMENTIERES. Shelled intermittently during day with 5.9s with V.guns otherwise quiet.	WWM
	7/8/17		Our operations. Patrols. One Patrol 1 NCO & 4 ORs. near Enemy wire, but returned on information received. 1 NCO & 10 ORs. left our lines to reconnoitre ditches in N.M.L. Artillery fires during day — Retaliation. Aircraft active all day. General Quiet period. Enemy Operations. A very quiet period. General Patrol Nayad 9AM Enemy discharged S'pinoid shells on our left. They burst in thick black smoke, dropping a calcite white light which continued to burn for 20-30 seconds after bursting. The forward ground officers of these which emerge the smell of gas retired, & it is thought that they were retired from T.M's	WWM

1875 Wt. W593/826 1,000,000 1/15 J.B.C. & A. A.D.S.S./Forms/C. 2118.

WAR DIARY
or
INTELLIGENCE SUMMARY

of the 2/10 (SCOTTISH) KINGS (Liverpool) Regt

Army Form C. 2118

(Erase heading not required.)

Instructions regarding War Diaries and Intelligence Summaries are contained in F.S. Regs., Part II. and the Staff Manual respectively. Title Pages will be prepared in manuscript.

Place	Date	Hour	Summary of Events and Information	Remarks and references to Appendices
BOIS GRENIER Brech. Bois Sub Sector Map reference 36 N.W.4 7A	8/8/17		Our Operations. Patrol. A Patrol left T.3.1.c at 10 p.m. returned at 12.25 a.m. Reported Enemy covering party to a working party at T.2.1.C.4.1. Owing to a broad ditch stream in between, our Patrol was unable to there on this party. Artillery fired in Retaliation on W.2 MACQUART &c and covering fire to T.M. Shoots. Round. Very Quiet Period. Enemy-shelling. Artillery Quiet. Maximum Aircraft. Fairly active in patrolling & reconnaissance.	MNM
	9/8/17		Our Operations. Patrols. A covering party lay out in front of RONSARTS to protect a working party. Found absence of Enemy Artillery fire during night. Artillery active in Retaliation during day. Aircraft active patrolling. General quiet period. Enemy Operations Artillery. Been seen fairly still. Considerable Enemy registration on our Sector 10th 7.7 p.m. throughout the day. Otherwise quiet day.	MNM
	10/8/17		Our Operations Patrol. Our Patrol left our lines during 8. Wth. returned without seeing or hearing anything of the Enemy. Artillery Very active in response to S.O.S. between 8.50 & 10 p.m. Thereafter fairly quiet day. Aircraft Patrolling as usual. None active in enemy. Enemy Operations. Artillery. From 7.45 p.m. approximately as Enemy put down a barrage on our FL. +S. in our Sector which lasted for half an hour after a break of about 15 minutes a most intense drum-fire was placed on FL + S. + CTs. This lasted for two hours. Trench Pd and M.G. bombardment Enemy Bossed out with Manns of all Calibres including Runn. Jars + Pine Apples, lettz/ feat mostly affected. During the barrage Enemy entered our lines. A Bomb. detached suffered heavily. Bomb. also seen. Officers were found in front line. A Stokes Gun in M.1. 3 mg. Casualties 1 Of (and Off Parsons B.E.) Killed, 2 OR Wounded	MNM

WAR DIARY or INTELLIGENCE SUMMARY

Army Form C. 2118

of the 2/10 (SCOTTISH) KINGS (Liverpool Regt)

Place	Date	Hour	Summary of Events and Information	Remarks and references to Appendices
BOIS GRENIER Rue du Bois Sub Sector	11/8/17		Operations. Artillery. Quiet during day. Aircraft. Very great patrolling between activity throughout the day.	WDHM
Map Reference 36.N.W.4. T.A.	12/8/17		Enemy Operations. Artillery. Enemy appeared to be registering on line in front of Subsidiary Line, in front of Sugar Box & left of Rennes. Aircraft. Fairly active during day.
Our Operations. A Wiring Patrol left our lines from ENFERS FARM Salient. Wiring encountered from 1.15 AM to 1.35 AM. Enemy trumpeted and left Sector in vicinity of CHARD's CRATER, both sides of Rabbit & Minnie. Casualties 3 O.R's killed (2 2/4 Suffolks) & O.R. wounded. Sgts Artillery responded 1.20 a.m. at 1.25 AM stopped for about 25 minutes.
Artillery. Quiet during day. Aircraft. Great patrolling activity. General. Quiet period.
Enemy Operations. Fairly quiet period. Aircraft. Active patrolling & recoy.
Battn relieved by 2/4th South Lancs Regt. Relief completed by 11.30 p.m. D. Cos remained in Subsidiary Line as S.R. Bn.	WDHM
ERQUINGHEM	13/8/17 14/8/17 15/8/17 16/8/17		A Coy relieved D Coy in Subsidiary Line as S.R. Coy. Presentation of Ribands to members of Battalion by Lieut A Gemmell joined from 3rd R.B. Battn & posted to A Coy. Exchanges of Capt. & Lieut ? RWF & Lt Battn to take in charge of Capt. B3.B2. RWF Coy in Command of 2/9 K.L.R.	WDHM
	17/8/17		Bullets, Usual Training, Working Parties etc	
	18/8/17		Transport Inspection by C.O.	
	19/8/17			
	20/8/17		ERQUINGHEM Shelled during afternoon & evening. About 30 shells fell between 6 & 7pm. Several the streets were obstructed at 8.10pm. 2 Civilians killed (one woman & 1 nurse), several others wounded. Battn relieved 2/14 Battn South Lancs Regt in Rue du Bois Sub Sector. Relief Completed 11.30 p.m.	

1875 Wt. W593/826 1,000,000 4/15 J.B.C. & A. A.D.S.S./Forms/C. 2118.

WAR DIARY
of 1st Bn 2/10 (Scottish) King's (Liverpool) Regt
INTELLIGENCE SUMMARY

Army Form C. 2118

(Erase heading not required.)

Place	Date	Hour	Summary of Events and Information	Remarks and references to Appendices
BOIS GRENIER	21/8/17		Our Operations – Patrols listening patrols lay out in front of PEAR TREE FARM & WILLOW GAP. Nothing special to report.	
Rue du Bois Sub Sector			Artillery Enemy fire for the H/T.M.Bn. Shoots + in retaliation for Minnies, otherwise quiet. H.T.M.B. fired 10 rounds between 3 + 4 pm on to Enemy Support. With moderate effect.	MMM
Map Reference 36 NW 4 7A			Aircraft Very active throughout the day.	
			Enemy Operations Artillery About 70.4.22 RH on FL + S between COWGATE + WINE AV. Grenadiers 2 killed (L.H? Batn.) 4th Batt. (L.P.?) 2 wounded (C.Q.). Otherwise fairly quiet. Aircraft Considerable activity. Enemy planes kept at a great height.	
	22/8/17		Our Operations Patrols 1 NCO + 2 men left WINE AV at 1 AM to examine wire cut by MTM Party found retaining wire. Patrol returned. LG fire was brought to bear on position. A protective patrol lay out in front of CHARD'S FARM. Working parties located + LG fire brought to bear in Rear.	MMM
			Artillery 18-Pounders fired in retaliation to Minnies which were more active than usual. Aircraft Considerable patrolling work during day. General fairly quiet period.	
			Enemy Operations Artillery 4.2". About 10 PEAR TREE GAP 303" About 40 WINE AV + COWGATE Supports. Minnies on FISHER'S Supports + COWGATE to WINE AV. Aircraft Considerable hostile patrolling during day.	
	23/8/17		Our Operations Patrols One Patrol 1/NCO + 5 ORs left COWGATE & proceeded across NML toward inversion where Enemy burying party was observed. Patrol came under hostile fire and drew to our lines, bringing LG fire to bear on the party. HQR C/P CHARD'S FARM at 1.30 AM. Two Enemy burying parties located + M.G. fire brought to bear on them. Artillery fired in retaliation during day. Aircraft fairly active but rarely fair weather restricted our Patrol work. General Quiet weather. Good deal more activity on High Ridge.	MMM
			Enemy Operations Artillery showed increased activity. 4.2" 142" in support + Sub Sid line and woods in Rear. Some WELLINGTON AV & TEITH WALK. Aircraft Less active than usual.	

1875 Wt. W593/826 1,000,000 4'15 J.B.C. & A. A.D.S.S./Forms/C. 2118.

WAR DIARY

of the 2/10 (Scottish) Kings (Liverpool) Regt

Army Form C. 2118

INTELLIGENCE SUMMARY

(Erase heading not required.)

Place	Date	Hour	Summary of Events and Information	Remarks and references to Appendices
BOIS GRENIER Rue du Bois Sub Sector Nof Riverine B6kw4 7A	24/8/17		Our operations. Patrols were out. Artillery. Own Retaliation. Income Incidents & Incident Supports. Enemy fire for M.T.M.B. Shots. M.T.M.Bs fired 30 Rounds between 1.30 & 2.45 p.m. on wire INCIDENT TRENCH & front Support. Retaliation heavy 40 4·2" Many 3·03" & 5" Minnies. Aircraft None seen active owing to bad weather. Enemy operations Artillery H.V. gun. Some on WYNNE Av. 4·2" WYNE to COWGATE AV. 10 COWGATE kwb. 12 WELLINGTON Av. 3·03" 60 Supports Rue du Bois salient to WYNNE AV. MINNIES 5" WYNE AV. Aircraft Inactive owing to weather.	WMM
	25/8/17		Our operations. Patrols 1 Officer & 10 ORs left 4P & COWGATE at 1·10AM re-examined wire but no Germans. Patrols fully completed. Artillery. 18 Pdrs. fired in retaliation 4 T.M.s during day. Wire reported fairly damaged. Artillery. 18 Pdrs. fired in retaliation & for Enemy fire fr x.63. H.T.M.B. INCOMPLETE Supports, Aircraft Fairly active on Patrol work. General Very quiet period. Enemy operations Artillery 4·2 & 8 on WYNE AV 15 Heavy Minnies & Supports, 12 Willow Av Supports. Aircraft Less active than usual. General Much quieter period.	WMM
	26/8/17		Our operations Artillery Retaliation. INCOMPLETE & COWGATE & Covering fire Ln H.T.M.B. Aircraft active. Artillery - General Very Quiet period. Enemy operations 5·9s 15" WELLINGTON AV. Patrols 3·03" 6·2 and 5·0 WYNE to Support & Rue du Bois Salient. Aircraft Fairly active during day. General Very quiet. The quietest day for a long time.	WMM
	27/8/17		Our operations. Patrols 0 Listening Post lay out in N.M.L. Rue du Bois Salient. Report that enemy ignited a man wire heavy Wire. Artillery. Very quiet during the whole day. Aircraft Very little activity owing to bad weather. General. A very quiet period. Enemy operations. Very little activity generally. At 5·15 am 3 men were fired at in N.M.L. offsite Willow Locality. Two escaped to safety and 1 left. 3 Prussian prisoners. Should own area to fire knowledge of our totally committed & turned to the Rue du Bois, were stood to... Mound his evacuated team two exchanges went to offer to fire an account of himself. He soon fired ...	WMM

WAR DIARY

or INTELLIGENCE SUMMARY

of the 2/10th (SCOTTISH) KINGS (Liverpool) Regt.

Army Form C. 2118

Place	Date	Hour	Summary of Events and Information	Remarks and references to Appendices
BOIS GRENIER Rue du Bois Sub Sector Map Reference 36 N.W. 4 TA	28/8/17		Our Operations. Patrols 1 NCO & 5 men left our lines at WINTON AV. & made careful search of the locality where the third Russian prisoner was reported to have been seen, but no trace of him could be found. Artillery fire very covering fire to TMB shorts. Aircraft practically nil during the day, owing to bad weather generally. Light shell & rifle fire during greater part of day. A very quiet period. Enemy Operations. Artillery 4.2: 10 Rue du Bois Salient to WINE AV. FL. TMs. 4 Heavy currents & Medium head of WINE AV. (Signallers dug out smashed. Instruments damaged) (Thermite very quiet period. Battn relieved by 2/4 South Lancashire Regt. Relief completed 10:50 p.m. B Co + 1 Platoon D Co. left in the line.	W/War.
ERQUINGHEM	29/8/17		Billets. Baths. Kit Inspections etc. Capt. H.T. WHITSON reported for duty from Divisional HQrs. & took over command of A. Coy.	W/War.
	30/8/17			W/War.
	31/8/17		Billets. Usual Training. Working parties etc.	

35807. W16879/M1879 500,000 3/17 F.T. (1074) Forms/W3091/3   Army Form W.3091.

Cover for Documents.

Nature of Enclosures.

War Diary
2/10 King's Liverpool Regt

Notes, or Letters written.

WAR DIARY or INTELLIGENCE SUMMARY

Army Form C. 2118

of the 2/10 (Scottish) Kings (Liverpool Regt)

(Erase heading not required.)

Place	Date	Hour	Summary of Events and Information	Remarks and references to Appendices
ERQUINGHEM	1/9/17		A Coy relieved B Coy as S.A. Coy in the line.	Nil
	2/9/17		Billets. Usual training & working parties	Nil
	3/9/17			Nil
	4/9/17			
	5/9/17		Batt. relieved 2/4 South Lancs Regt in Rue du Bois Sub Sector. Relief completed 10.40 p.m. A Coy left, C Coy centre, D Coy Right, B. Battalion in line	Nil
BOIS GRENIER Map ref. Sheet 36 N.W.4 7.A	6/9/17		Our operations. Patrols. 3 Officer Patrols lay out in front of Gate in N.M.L. Everything reported quiet. Artillery 18 Pdrs fired destructive shoot Camouflage Screen ← INCLEMENT TRENCH & in Retaliation during day. The enemy fired M.T.M.B. Short M.T.M.B. fired 65 rounds during afternoon. Aircraft Very active during early part of the day. Enemy operations Artillery quiet. T.M. Heavy 10 Wine A.V. Medium 65 Cowgate & Wine Light 25 Cowgate & Wine. General Quiet Period.	Nil
	7/9/17		Our Operations Patrols. 1 N.C.O. + 5 men left Head of Sap at 2.55 A.M. for purpose of reconnoitring enemy Sap at I.21.b.80.35 (INCLEMENT TRENCH). They reached Enemy wire but could not locate the Sap. Returned at 4.30 A.M. 1 Officer + 10 men lay up in N.M.L. opposite Rue du Bois Salient but no contact with enemy was obtained. Artillery 18 Pdrs. Destructive Shoot. INCLEMENT TRENCH, INCISION & in Retaliation. T.M. Medium fired 50 rounds. Between 4-5 p.m. on to INCIDENT TRENCH. Effective Shoot. EFL herded in two places. 1 man 1/2 Cas fire after 50 rounds owing to 2 O.R.'s being wounded & a third man buried. Retaliation heavy. Enemy Operations Artillery 4.2" 40 Willow & Wine. 40 ENARDS FARM. 20 Cowgate & Wine Rd. 3.0.3" 15 Wine & Leith walk 30 Cowgate & Wine. 40 Chards Farm. Thg Heavy 24 Chards Farm, Cowgate. Medium 30 Enards Farm 40 Cowgate & Avondale. Light 50 Cow Gate. Aircraft. Some air raids over our lines during day. Flying H/h General Hostile Artillery & T.M's. have been active in Sub Sector. Fire being much concentrated on Chards Farm, Cowgate locality from Wine and T.M Covered out a very effective shoot on INCIDENT TRENCH. Otherwise the Sector lasted quietly	Nil

WAR DIARY / INTELLIGENCE SUMMARY

Army Form C. 2118

of the 2/10 (Scottish) King's (Liverpool) Regt.

Place	Date	Hour	Summary of Events and Information	Remarks and references to Appendices
BOIS GRENIER Rue du Bois Sub-Sector Map Reference 36.N.W.4. T.14.	8/9/17		Our operations. Patrols. 2 Patrols laid out in N.M.L. in front of new wire opposite COWGATE & WINE Avs. All returned quiet. Heavy ground mist in N.M.L. Artillery 18 pdrs. Destructive shoots - Areas F22c55.02 (very effective - many direct hits - huts damaged - material thrown up & left uncovered) INCOMPLETE AVENUE from I26d.69+9 & I27c.68.07 - causing fire for TMs. TMs x 57 M.T.M.B fired 91 rounds between 1 and 2pm on to wire and trench (INCLEMENT) - trench and parapet damaged. Enemy operations. Artillery 6.4.2s WINE AVENUE 3.03s 20 apple SALOP WINE 30 salvoing and bursts in or near HAYSTACK & WINE TMs. Heavy 12 WINE - Some pineapples in WINE LOCALITY. Aircraft. Some slight hostile activity during day. General Very quiet front - During the night enemy bombed his own wire and sent up a large number of very lights - over 18 between 9 TMs fairly active.	PW
	9/9/17		Our operations. Patrol left WINE ST & examined enemy wire cut by TMs - Found uncut except opposite trench in centre of GAZETTE DES ARDENNES front in N.M.L. featured to top of fines opposite fighting strives in general. Artillery 18 pdrs destructive shoots. INDEX DRIVE INCONSISTENT RESERVE & INCOMPLETE SUPPORT. 4.5 HoWs destructive shoot. INCOMPLETE SUPPORT - Normal at I22c53.10. TMs x 63 M.T.M.B. fired 153 rounds between 4.30 & 8 PM on head of INCOMPLETE LANE - opportunity shoot - light retaliation. MGs indirect fire at night in rear areas. Enemy operations. Artillery 30 59s CHAPELLE 42 RUERIES - MGs front at aeroplanes during day. General inactivity much improved. On whole - TMs very active, enemy artillery before & trench mortars. Very little shelling of our trench systems reported.	PW
	10/9/17		Our operations. Patrols - Normal patrols If 10 PP - 20 men party in gaps. Artillery 15 pdrs fired as follows - Burst function and tangent I326 70.65. New work at LA HOUSSIE - M shields. INCISION INCISION INCOMPLETE SUPPORTS - causing his new TMs - 4.5 HoWs destructive shoot from bulging I342 25.15 (good shoot heavy direct hits. INDEX TRENCH SUPPORTS. MGs front 2/000 rounds. TMs Harrison fired 10 rounds on enemy front areas. Aircraft Very active. General Both sides now active with artillery but TMs. Major RHM Maxwell left for training class at FLECHIN.	PW

WAR DIARY
or
INTELLIGENCE SUMMARY
(Erase heading not required.)

Army Form C. 2118

Instructions regarding War Diaries and Intelligence Summaries are contained in F.S. Regs, Part II. and the Staff Manual respectively. Title Pages will be prepared in manuscript.

Place	Date	Hour	Summary of Events and Information	Remarks and references to Appendices
BOIS GRENIER	11/9/17		No operations. Patrols - usual battle patrols of 1 officer and 10 O.R. being out in 9 of the during night.	
RUE DU BOIS SUB SECTOR			Artillery. 18 pdr destructive shoots on OIL AVENUE - Retaliation. INCLEMENT INCIDENT INCH INCISION Trenches - 4.5 Hows. Destructive shoot - Road at LE BAS HAU. TMS fired 90 rounds on INCLUDE SUPPORTS and INCONSISTENT trench. (effective shoot) M.G's usual indirect fire at night on trust areas. Lines been opened for 15 minutes in response to S.O.S. call from PARK ROW.	Mil
MAP REF 36 NW 4 7A			Enemy artillery 10 4.2s COWGATE 40 CHARDS FARM. 3.0 3s 110 CHARDS FARM. SO WINE & ORCHARD.	
			TMs heavy SAFETY ALLEY. Nothing to COWGATE 10 CHARDS FM. Aircraft fairly active. General. Our artillery and TMs active. Enemy shows some increase in artillery and T.M. fire.	
	12/9/17		No operations. Patrols usual battle patrols being out in quota. Artillery 18 pdr carried out destructive shoots also 4.5 Hows - on INCIDENT TR and INCLEMENT TRENCH. TMs Heavies fired 10 rounds on INCLEMENT TRENCH. LA MOUSSOIE - Enemy operations. Artillery - 4.2s on CHARDS FARM & LEITH WALK also 50 3.0 3s TMs 12 minnenos on COWGATE General fairly quiet period.	Mil
	13/9/17		No operations. Usual battle patrols being up intensive gaps. Artillery 18 pdrs + Hows. Destructive shoots on INCLINE and INCENCE AVENUES. Retaliation INCLEMENT SUPPORTS. TMs Heavies fired 10 rounds on INDEX SUPPORTS. Aircraft active patrolling our line. Enemy artillery - TMs very little on this sector. Aircraft one plane flying low over our lines during T.M. shoot on night. General our quiet. Battn relieved by 2/4 LR and - C Coy in line as SR Coy.	Mil
ERQUINGHEM	14/9/17			9 Mil
	15/9/17		15/9/17. D Coy relieved C Coy as SR Coy in line	Mil
	16/9/17		Battn - usual training and musketry practices.	Mil

Army Form C. 2118

WAR DIARY
or
INTELLIGENCE SUMMARY
(Erase heading not required.)

Instructions regarding War Diaries and Intelligence Summaries are contained in F. S. Regs., Part II. and the Staff Manual respectively. Title Pages will be prepared in manuscript.

Place	Date	Hour	Summary of Events and Information	Remarks and references to Appendices
ERQUINGHEM	17/9/17		Batt'n relieved by 13th R.W.F. marched to ESTAIRES. D Coy relieved 8 P.M.	W.L
ESTAIRES	18/9/17		D Coy arrived ESTAIRES 3.30 A.M. Batt'n rested for day.	W.L
BAS RIEUX	19/9/17		Batt'n marched to BAS RIEUX - Billets for 200 men only - Remainder of Batt'n bivouaced	W.L
FLECHIN	20/9/17		Batt'n marched to FLECHIN	W.L
FLECHIN	21-9-17 to 30-9-17		Bn forms part of a unit in Army Reserve - Training	W.L

(signature) Lt. Col.
Cmdg 2/10 4th (Scottish) Bn The K.L.R.

WAR DIARY
INTELLIGENCE SUMMARY

Army Form C. 2118

2/10 Liverpool Regt
Vol 9

Place	Date October 1917	Hour	Summary of Events and Information	Remarks and references to Appendices
FLECHIN	1/7		Training	W
	8		Inspection at AUCHY AU BOIS by Commander-in-chief Sir Douglas Haig	W
	9/17		Training	W
	18		Left FLECHIN - Battn marched to COMPERDU - Billeted for the night.	W
COMPERDU	19		Batn. proceeded to PROVEN by motor buses. Arrived 7 P.M. Proceeded to PURBROOK CAMP	W
PROVEN			Arrived 9.30 P.M. Men very exhausted	W
	19/23		Cleaning up and training	W
	24		Batn moved to POODLE CAMP, PROVEN. In reserve (Divisional)	W
	25		Cleaning up	W
ELVERDINGE	26/27		Battn entrained at midnight for ELVERDINGE. Arrived 3 A.M. marched to WOLFE CAMP - MALAKOFF AREA.	W
	28/31		Training - Cleaning up - Reconnaissances by Officers and N.C.O.S - Bombs dropped from enemy aeroplanes on this area nightly - 2 O.R. and 7 horses slightly wounded.	W

[signature] Lt Col
Comdg 2/10 (Scottish) Bn The K.L.R.

WAR DIARY or INTELLIGENCE SUMMARY

Army Form C. 2118

1/10 Liverpool R.
Vol 16

Place	Date Nov 1917	Hour	Summary of Events and Information	Remarks and references to Appendices
ELVERDINGHE	1		At WOLFE CAMP, MALAKOFF AREA. Cleaning up	HW
LANGEMARCK	2		Battalion left WOLFE CAMP by road and marched to HUDDLESTON CAMP. Marched off 9AM, arrived 10.30 AM. Battalion left Camp at 4.30 PM along duckboard tracks A and B to EAGLE TRENCH about 500 yards beyond LANGEMARCK. Relieved 9.30 P.M. 2/5th K.L.R. Capt D Gray and Lt Morris and Capt Roberts bivouacked in bunks in support. A and B Coys under Lt Stead and Capt Saunders moved up to close supports on a line through old Rlwy about 1200 yards in front of EAGLE TRENCH. Battn H.Q. at pill box DOUBLE COT'S behind EAGLE TRENCH. Enemy shelling with H.E. moderate – 12 minenwerfers & 2 AM heavy Gas bombardment.	HW
	3		Work of consolidation carried on – Saunders and shell holes improved. – Enemy shelling not heavy during day. S.O.S. Enemy shelling in support this night no attack materialised. Gas bombardment carried out over RZ EAGLE TRENCH from 1 – 2AM these 800 yards have put up stout fighting in front of EAGLE TRENCH. Dugouts little – Trenches improved.	HW
	4		Relieved by 2/4th S.Lancs. Proceeded to front line and relieved 2/9 K.L.R. Relief completed 12 midnight. Dispositions. D.B.A in front line with C Coy in support. One half retained in support at GRAVEL FARM. W & left to REQUETE FARM in night. Still two occupied. Batts H.Q. at LOUIS FARM (pill box). Enemy shelling with H.E. rather go from 4 PM to 4 AM. An artillery put Boys heavy barrage on enemy F.L. at 5AM. which continued until 6AM. Consolidation and wiring carried on – Relieved by 7/4th S.Lancs. Relief completed 10 PM. Batts proceeded to HUDDLESTON CAMP, near CANAL BANK where night was spent. Rest.	HW
	5			HW
ELVERDINGHE	6	7 A.M.	HUDDLESTON CAMP near CANAL BANK where night was spent. Rest. Relieved by 9th Battn East Riding Regt at 12 noon. Proceeded to BRIDGE CAMP. Marched to stations at ELVERDINGHE at 12 noon. Entrained and proceeded to AIDRICQ. arrived 6 P.M. Marched to L'STERGAUX – ZUTKERQUE.	HW
	7			HW 10.X. 2 sheets HW

WAR DIARY
INTELLIGENCE SUMMARY

Place	Date	Hour	Summary of Events and Information	Remarks and references to Appendices
ZUTKERQUE	7/30		Butts - Training. During tour of duty from 27th to 11th inst. over 150 bodies were buried by this battalion - These included despatch Highlanders, Rifle Brigade, London Regt, Norfolks, Cavalry, Royal North Lancs. A number of German bodies were also buried. Investigation was promoted to the proper quarter. Casualties O.R. Killed 8 Died of Wounds 1 Wounded 34 Sick 16 / 59	

Hamilton Capt.

WAR DIARY or INTELLIGENCE SUMMARY

Army Form C. 2118.

of 2/1st (Hertford) Nurse (Cyclist) Bn

Place	Date	Hour	Summary of Events and Information	Remarks and references to Appendices
LUTRERQUE	4/8/17		Billets - Main Body returned from leave, left for Divine Schl	
	5/8/17		Training	
HERZEELE	6/8/17		Left LUTRERQUE 5.30 A.M. marched to AUDRICQ entrained at 7 A.M. arrived PROVEN 11 A.M. marched to HERZEELE arrived 2.30 P.M.	
	7/8/17		Billets. Training - A + C Coys Transport & Vickers Tms B + D Coys & Lewis Gun Sections	
	8/8/17		"	
	9/8/17		"	
	10/8/17		" Lt Col M.P. Boyle V.D. MC ? Hutchin ? ? ? ? took over command	
	11/8/17		"	
	12/8/17		"	
	13/8/17		" Inspection of Equipment by the G.O.C. Brigade	
	14/8/17		"	
	15/8/17		" 2nd Lieut H. Henderson Joined Batt. from 3rd Batt ? ? ?	
	16/8/17		" Rain all morning - Afternoon Batt ? ? ? ? ? ?	
	17/8/17		20" Essex arr. in 16 Billets	
	18/8/17		Batt. to HERZEELE 12.30. Brit. from HERZEELE 3 p.m.	

Army Form C. 2118.

WAR DIARY
of the 2/10 (Scottish) Bat. Kings (Liverpool) Reg.
INTELLIGENCE SUMMARY.
(Erase heading not required.)

Place	Date	Hour	Summary of Events and Information	Remarks and references to Appendices
ELVERDINGHE	24/7/17 – 26/7/17		WSwct Training Heat wet	
(EMILE LARRY CAMP)	27/7/17		Batt. Comdr & Batt. Mnrched to Canal Bank md Rd Belgium/600 Stories B & a 7.3 Western	
			relieved the 2/6 K.LR in Support Front & Secor et	
	28/7/17		Working Parties serving Main Defence Line & Cooking Packs Forward	
CANAL BANK	28/7/17		S.O.S. about 8.30am Batt. Stood to for one hour then back	
	29/7/17			
	29/7/17		Batt. relieved 2/4 K.L.R. in front line as left Batt. Details front	
			Railway Camp then in Reliefs and took up	
			C Coy. Left Front Line. B Coy. Right Front Line & Pats. A Coy. Support	
			Yser Bend B. Reserve at Cranside Batt. found the usual working parties	
			Reports 10 Wagon lines at Battalion Camp at 5.15pm over one hour cont.	
	30/7/17		Front line & system nearly 700 yds meters Van...	
	31/7/17		Zero hour 3.50am. Captured Antwerp D.B. B.C. relieved	

WAR DIARY
or
INTELLIGENCE SUMMARY

Army Form C. 2118.

(Erase heading not required.)

Instructions regarding War Diaries and Intelligence Summaries are contained in F. S. Regs., Part II. and the Staff Manual respectively. Title pages will be prepared in manuscript.

Place	Date	Hour	Summary of Events and Information	Remarks and references to Appendices
In the Field	29/9/18		Mar Ph. BIXCHOOTE WOODS. Battalion left CANAL BANK CAMP & left B.S. & 7.3 BELGIUM Sheet 28 NW Bdn 6H at 7.30pm on the following order. Bn HQ. O.D.A.B – Kellium right Bn K-L R– HOUTHULST FOREST left sub sector. Map ref. BIXCHOOTE WOOD 20 SW Bn 6A U.6.d.6.9 to U.5.6 3.6 Relief Completed 2am. Disposition D. Coy in right C Coy on left in front line. A Coy in support at VEE BEND B Coy in reserve at CAROUNE FARM. No Patrols sent out owing to full moon and enemy working lights too strong.	
	30/9/18		Quiet morning. In the evening on our right flank 75th Bn Lahore Force attacked TURENNE CROSSING COLOBRI FARM and gained VR.7.5.60 and VL D.00.55. Barrage started from 8 pm to 8 pm to operate with MG and rifle fire. Large amount of enemy shifting on retaliation. 2 casualties. 1 D Coy was taken by 25th Bn Scott Fames. L.O. Caserne. Also Regular to supply working party for 25th Bn South Lanc. Sent Platoon of A Coy — put out [illegible] to remove wounded — Gunner's Same. No time to our front. Manby Forth 1 Patrol 1 Officer and 4 men succeeded in front of our Right Post. No enemy encountered	
	31/9/18	5 am	Heavy artillery fire about 2 miles away on right 90's sent up from that direction. Quickly shelling. Sent ... and MG fire ... on back slave. No aircraft activity. Our down – Enemy in front. Patrols. Patrols (1) 1 Officer and 3 men accompanied [illegible] Right Post Coy 1 NCO & 3 men. Reconnoissance up to and left post — Nothing [illegible] of enemy — [illegible] very [illegible] – very [illegible] difficult owing to moon on fugen known.	
	1/10/18		Great Morning. Good visibility. Sam aircraft [illegible] Battery work. Aircraft active on both sides. Patrols. Patrols to recce position left front of own enemy post of 30 recce moving across Batt. front to Kellium. Remnant Battalion on left. No contact with enemy. Shell burst at door of Ay. Hg. 1 man killed 2 Officers slightly wounded	
	2/10/18	5.25am	Artillery fire in the field. Short for a few of Moy. Low visibility – [illegible] movement slightly on left. Advancing into the [illegible] Bn HQ. right in right front loc in front in [illegible] followed by 7th Bn K.L. Rifles. [illegible] enabled 8.30 am Heavy Ag (8) relatively Low Casualties. Bn HQ Pentionens B.5.55.05 at 9.20 am. Arrived H. farm A.13.a.0.2. 2.30 am. Total Casualties. 2 killed 14 wounded	

Wt. W14422/M1160 350,000 12/16 D.D. & L. Forms/C/2118/14.

WAR DIARY
INTELLIGENCE SUMMARY

of the 2/10 (Scottish) Kings (Liverpool) Regt

Army Form C. 2118.

(Erase heading not required.)

Place	Date	Hour	Summary of Events and Information	Remarks and references to Appendices
H CAMP (A6a02)	3/1/18		Kit Inspections & cleaning up. Surplus Transport left by road for STEENWERCK	RM
	4/1/18		Batt. entrained at INTERNATIONAL CORNER 8.30 AM Arrived BAILLEUL 11.30 AM Marched to HOLLEBECQUE CAMP nr STEENWERCK. Transport entrained 11.30 AM arrived in Camp 6 pm	RM
HOLLEBECQUE CAMP	5/1/18		Kit Inspection & cleaning up	MR
	6/1/18		Training	MR
	7/1/18		Bn Baths. Training.	MR
	8/1/18		Training	MR
	9/1/18		"	MR
	10/1/18		Very bad weather. Johnstones Day kept. Dinners indents. Officers Sergts waiting on the men. Casualties McDonald "A" Coy, Gregory E. Coy.	SM
	11/1/18		Working party called for. 300 strong to wire between HOUPLINES & WEST YORKS. 4 Casualties MG fire	MM
	12/1/18		A start made under Pioneer Sgt to strengthen huts against Bombs. Working party out again 150 strong	MM
ERQUINGHEM	13/1/18		Bn moved up to Subsidiary line. Bn HQ ERQUINGHEM Road Railway Crossing Relieved 7/4 KRR	MR
	14/1/18		Bn on working Parties (morning to 4 pm)	MM
	15/1/18		Bn on Working parties. "Details" left out to Baths.	MM
	16/1/18		Bn on Working Parties (morning to 4 pm)	MM
	17/1/18		Bn on Working parties. Relief orders cancelled. Relief next 18/1/19	MM

WAR DIARY
INTELLIGENCE SUMMARY

Army Form C. 2118.

2/10th (Scottish) Kings L'pool Regt.

Place	Date	Hour	Summary of Events and Information	Remarks and references to Appendices
HOUPLINES SECTOR	18/1/18		The Bn. relieved 1/5 S.R. in this sector. Relief was completed about midnight. Col. Brodie visited B. Coy. Conditions very bad. No communication trenches 4 ft 6" of water in many trenches — In line B, C, D. Support A.	M
	19/1/18		Col. Brodie visited C. Coy in the morning & D Coy in the afternoon. About 3.30 pm. Two 2" mortars 'B' Coy had two minnies & Spence wounded. 2 O/R killed and 3 wounded. This brot. was invalid. During the night our artillery retaliated satisfactorily. 1 O/R wounded slightly by enemy sniper. Weather conditions good, warm, no rain. Few shells on HOUPLINES.	1/5 M
	20/1/18		Brigade Scheme for alteration of this sector. Bn. in the Line carried out. Still no rain. A few shells on HOUPLINES. 173 M.G.C. carried out "Shoot" according to Divisional Scheme. M.G. Vickers & patrol section worked along No. mans land from Centre to left sector.	M

WAR DIARY
or
INTELLIGENCE SUMMARY.

Army Form C. 2118.

Place	Date	Hour	Summary of Events and Information	Remarks and references to Appendices
HOUPLINES SUB SECTOR	21/1/18		Relieved by 7/6th K.L.R. On reached HOLLEBEQUE CAMP about 11. P.M.	M
HOLLEBEQUE CAMP	22/1/18		General Barnes visited the camp to see new Foot washing Hut.	M
"	23/1/18		Corps Commander Inspected. Did not turn up.	M
"	24/1/18		Memo rec'd Oct AA. Heavy working parties on Corps Ammunition Defences	M
"	25/1/18		Look in camp on A.A. Protection. Working parties again on Corps Ammunition Defences.	M
"	26/1/18		Working parties again. Weather good.	M
"	27/1/18		C & D Coys on morning working parties. Relieved 7/6th K.L.R in Outerdown Line. H.Q. H.S.6.9.8.  Arrived at these H.Q. Ordered moved to relieve H.Q 2/K.S.L.R. in these. Relief complete 9.30 p.m.	M
HOUPLINES SUB SECTOR H.S. 6. 9. 8.	28/1/18		General Payter visited front two posts. Relieved by 1/K.S.L.R. H.Q. at 6 p.m.	M
"	29/1/18		Received S.O. 32 amendments.	M
"	30/1/18		Evidenced 1/KSLR in front line. 1 Coy 7/Ls in Outerdown Line. Dummy Raid. 9.4.5.16. 9.5. Artillery M.G + L.G Fire on central Trench.	M
"	31/1/18		Very misty all preparations for Bois O.P. No 37 canned out at 6.30 p.m. delayed at 8 cancelled. Peculiar guiet Day	M

WAR DIARY
or
INTELLIGENCE SUMMARY

2/10th (Scottish) Bn. The King's (L'pool Regt.)

Army Form C. 2118.

Vol 13

13 X
3 sheets

Place	Date	Hour	Summary of Events and Information	Remarks and references to Appendices
HOUPLINES SUB SECTOR	1/7/18		Day broke misty with a heavy frost all over the ground. These conditions prevailed throughout the day. Anything working our movements at Chevies Difficile. BN. order No 32 Circulated along to-day. About 11 am snipers fast to right of No 5 post sent a large part of posts retiring along ditch to Pt of Reines. Lewis gunner claimed a Handough Reported one of No 5 post cut. News/dispositions made - Sgt Jeffery wounded on [illegible] No 34 Zero hrs 8.30 pm - the News completed succession - slight casualty. cet[illegible]	
	2/7/18		[illegible] patrols. No attempt [illegible] said anywhere No 5 post. Consequently they now can intercept enemy. No 5 post visibility also given certain amount of courage but was E76.N.7.A. relieves top at night. The BN near HOLLEBERGS Camp at 10.30 p.m. on 2 ambulance lorries.	
	3/7/18		Be prepared under any arrangements. Inspection.	
	4/7/18		C'oy m/m Pls. OC Coy inspection rest sectn.	
	5/7/18		BN + C'D Coys moved to forward equipment. Coy '70' N.G.C attached 1/5 Coy inspector's list A. Coy on the Coys/hrs. At post 3pm platoon shellon NIEPPE. Two had messages showing 12 Battalion in ARMENTIERES. MAJ Thorn arrived to take up 2nd Command of BN.	
	6/7/18		Most effect billets we have been in.	
	7/7/18		Work same as yesterday. Large quantities of salvage refuse removed.	
L'EPINETTE SUB SECTOR	8/7/18		Relieved 1/4 K.S.L.R. in L'EPINE DE SUSSEX. Sectr. Enfield Posetion 2 platoons out all night. Speed 3 and No 2 bns. C/D Coy are disposed of between A B in post line 2 Coy 2/7/16 in intersay line.	

WAR DIARY
or
INTELLIGENCE SUMMARY
(10th (Scottish) Bn. The King's (L'pool Regt.)

Army Form C. 2118.

(Erase heading not required.)

Place	Date	Hour	Summary of Events and Information	Remarks and references to Appendices
ARMENTIERES SUB. SECTOR	9/2/18		The L'EPINETTE SUB. SECTOR was taken over by the ARMENT BRIGADE - SUB. SECTOR. Quiet day. Few shells burst on the outer my line about 3 pm. Night quiet. Had Zeppellin. No aerial activity.	BR.
	10/2/18		Weather quiet. A bright day with a fair amount of intermittent shelling. Very light. Enemy seen wiring in front of no stunt pay. One man killed. Several links & lineman being shot.	BR.
	11/2/18		Machine gun & Platoon of "A" Coy of the K.L.R. were shooting during the day. Rest inaudible. Relieved by B of the K.L.R. my complete 6 7 p.m.	BR.
			Outsel Deer men - interval officer & orderly room ptes. H.Q. O.S. office went to hut rifle & Lewis gun training platoon ERQUINGHEM	BR.
	12/2/18		Company N.C.O.S & officer went to Brigade demonstration Platoon H.A.C.	BR.
	13/2/18		Officers to N.C.O.S at ERQUINGHEM to demonstration platoon H.A.C. Reasonable amount of shell fire on the camp - remainder of pltn personnel employed Companies & training operating the normal front line duties of the [illegible]	BR.
	14/2/18		Bn. moved to DIEUE HERBOUN'S AREA ESTAIRES & Relieved Railway troops @ NIEPPE and Camps by the MT-R/V. Coy HQ at dispatch QPC new Bailleul Road. A & C Coys in Camps near Le Moyne area - "B" Coy [illegible] reserve at night.	M.
NEUF BERQUIN AREA	15/2/18		Day spent in settling into new Company	M.
	16/2/18			Par. 8354 Palmer Struck - returned Clermont Pkr.
	17/2/18		Spent digging to A [illegible] in [illegible] at 6 am	Pkr.
	18/2/18		Weather still fine & clean. "A" & "B" Coys carried out attachments to [illegible] Bdes at night	Pkr.
	19/2/18		Bn. not digging 8 am to 1 pm. C.O. reports 110 Coy. C.O B Coys. 3/8R attachments	Pkr.
	20/2/18		Digging and training	Pkr.
	21/2/18		[illegible]	Pkr.
	22/2/18		Commanding Officer proceeded to O.C. rifleman [illegible] home on command of Battn.	Pkr.

WAR DIARY
INTELLIGENCE SUMMARY

Army Form C. 2118.

Place	Date	Hour	Summary of Events and Information	Remarks and references to Appendices
NEAR DERNANCOURT	22/7/18		Inspection Ethernet Lewis Guns, Capt Thrumble, Capt Roe & Lt Robinson	1/22
	23/7/18		Bath Amusement Hotel at Vigne ESTAIRES. Guests Captain Huntly Ross & others	1/22
	24/7/18		Advanced Party Squadron	1/22
	25/7/18		Training. Pte companies meeting BM & to C.O. Insp.	1/22
	26/7/18		Inspecting Stables as usual. Inspection in preparation for C.O. Insp.	1/22
	27/7/18		Weekly wash & kit look over as usual	1/22
	28/7/18		Stables & inspections by L.O. Cruise Briggs	1/22
	29/7/18		Usual inspections	1/22

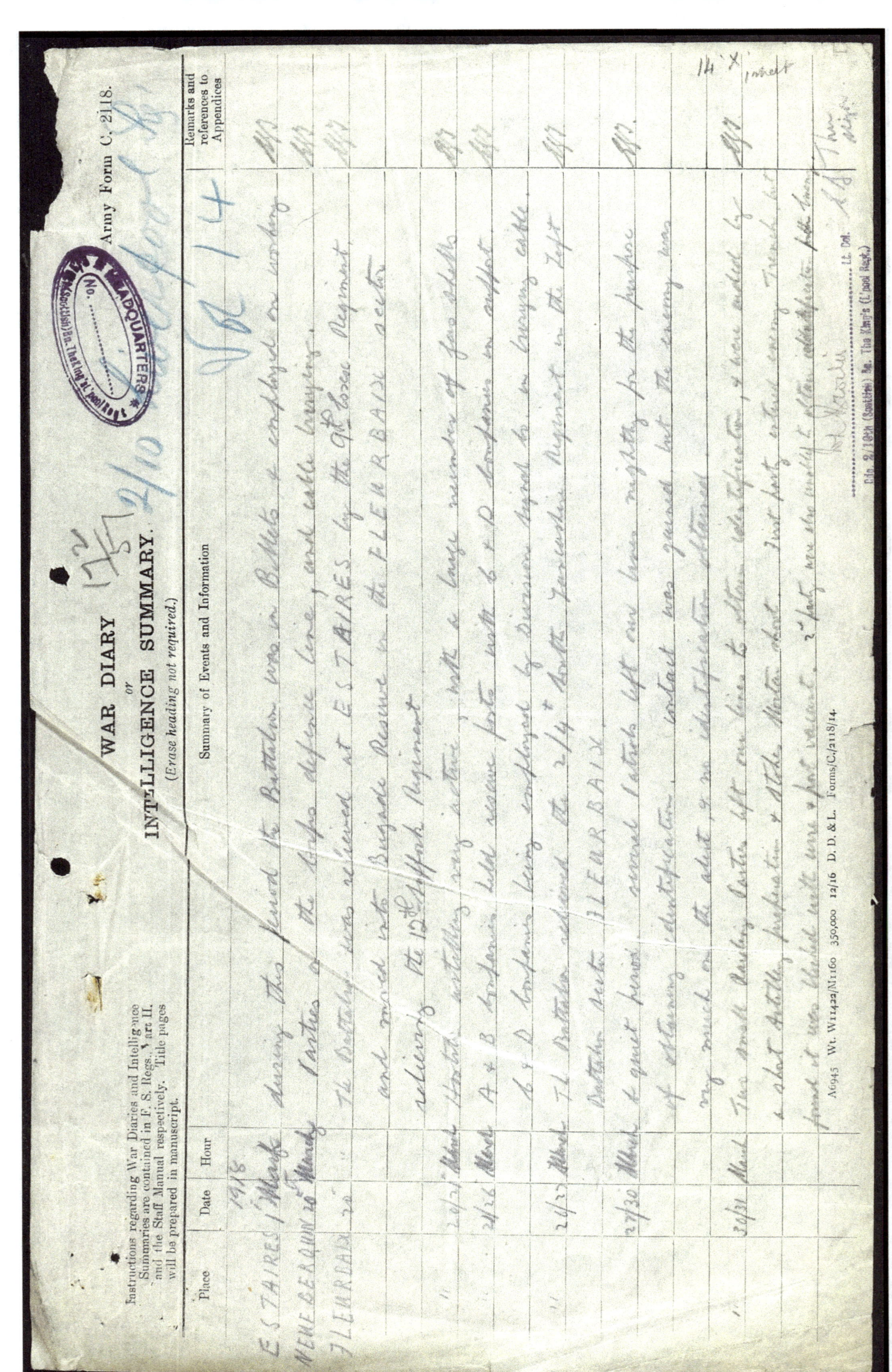

WAR DIARY or **INTELLIGENCE SUMMARY**
Army Form C. 2118.

Vol 14

Place	Date	Hour	Summary of Events and Information	Remarks and references to Appendices
ESTAIRES	19/18 1st March		During this period the Battalion was in Billets & employed on working parties on the Corps defence line, and cable laying.	893
MERE BERQUIN to Monday				893
FLEURBAIX	20th		The Battalion was relieved at ESTAIRES by the 9th Loyal Regiment and moved into Brigade Reserve in the FLEURBAIX sector relieving the 12th Suffolk Regiment	893
"	2/24th March		Hostile artillery very active, with a large number of gas shells	893
"	2/26 March		A & B Companies with reserve posts with C & D Companies in support	893
"	2/27 March		C & D Companies being employed by Division to dig communication cable	
"	2/29 March		The Battalion relieved the 2/4th North Lancashire Regiment in the Left Battalion sector FLEURBAIX	893
"	2/30 March		A quiet period occurred. Patrols left our lines nightly for the purpose of obtaining identifications contact was gained but the enemy were very much on the alert & no identification obtained	893
	2/31 March		Two small Raiding Parties left our lines to attempt identification, & were ousted by a shot Artillery preparation & other Mortar shoot. Both parts entered enemy Trenches but found it was held with no post present. 2 parts saw the enemy L. Gun detachments [...]	893

57th Division.
172nd Infantry Brigade
9-------

Battalion Disbanded 30.4.18.

2/10th BATTALION

THE KING'S LIVERPOOL REGIMENT

1st to 30th APRIL 1 9 1 8

Transferred to 55th Div 20.4.18.
Disbanded 30.4.18.

2/10 Liverpool

Vol 15

Rathbone Lt.

15 x
(2 sheet)

WAR DIARY
or
INTELLIGENCE SUMMARY
(Erase heading not required.)

Army Form C. 2118.

Place	Date	Hour	Summary of Events and Information	Remarks and references to Appendices
ESTAIRES	1/4/18		Bn marched from Estaires to Haverskerque.	
HAVERSKERQUE	2/4/18		Bn marched to Strenbecque and entrained there	
DOULLENS	3/4/18		Bn arrived Doullens 5.30 am and marched to Sus st Leger	
ST LEGER.	4/4/18		Training	
"	5/4		Bn moved at 8pm to Sombrin	
SOMBRIN	6/4		Training Major Tamplin 2nd i/c to Command	Major S. Ball 2nd/6th
"	7/4		arrived to take up appts of Battn.	
"	8/4		ditto	
FAMECHON	9/4		Bn moved at 9 am to FAMECHON.	
"	10/4		Training	
"	11/4		"	
SOMBRIN	12/4		Bn moved at 2pm back to SOMBRIN.	
PAS	13/4		Bn moved at 5.30 pm and marched into Bivouacs near PAS.	
"	14/4		By degrees notably 2/Lieuts arrived and until first Rft cards complete by 6pm.	
"	15/4			
HENU	16/4		Bn moved into billets at HENU	

A6945. Wt. W1422/M1160. 350,000 12/16 D.D. & L. Forms/C/2118/14.

Army Form C. 2118.

WAR DIARY
OR
INTELLIGENCE SUMMARY.
(Erase heading not required.)

Instructions regarding War Diaries and Intelligence Summaries are contained in F. S. Regs., Part II. and the Staff Manual respectively. Title pages will be prepared in manuscript.

Place	Date	Hour	Summary of Events and Information	Remarks and references to Appendices
HENU	17/4	—	(Reconnoitring and working and training. (Parties reconnoitred RED and PURPLE LINES.)	B Rathbone
"	18/4	—	} ditto	
"	19/4	—	} ditto	
"	20/4	—	Bn Entrained at 8 PM. Left for AUCHEL for transfer to 55th Divn (Amalgamation with 5 Staffs)	
BURBURE	21/4	—	Arrived AUCHEL 2 AM - went on to BURBURE - Rested during the day	
FESTUBERT	22/4	—	Bn inspected by Divr General at 11 AM. Proceeded into the line by companies of 6 Coy	
"	23/4		Renumbered as a separate unit in support.	
"	24/4		"B" Coy relieved X Coy 1st Bn in the KEEP. A relieved Y Coy in FESTUBERT. Coy by Coy took took up left front - D Coy close support	
"	25/4		C Coy relieved by S Staffs 1st Division.	
"	26/4		Bn Relieved by 6th Liverpools. Bn in Billets in LABOURSE	
LABOURSE	27/4		Billets slightly shelled during day	
"	28/4		Roads fairly heavily shelled during night	
VAUDRICOURT	29/4		Bn moved into the encampments at VAUDRICOURT	
"	30/4		1st 2nd Bns amalgamated. Bn struck 200 O/R's to 1st Bn. Remainder disbanded & drafted as follows. 70 O/R's 2 Officers to Amm Trans Comp 14 O/R's 401 others... 55th Divn Re inforcement Camp 14 O/R's...	On Reorganisation 8 WA 4 O + 2 (Scouts) for KLR 8 (Old Searchers) for KLR

A1045 Wt. W11422/M1160 350,000 12/16 D.D.&L. Forms/C/2118/14.

16TH DIVISION
47TH INFY BDE

2-10TH BN KING'S L'POOL REGT
MAY - JULY 1918

DISBANDED 3.8.18

47/16

Army Form C. 2118.

WAR DIARY
or
INTELLIGENCE SUMMARY.
(Erase heading not required.)

Army Form C. 2118.

TRAINING STAFF
2/10th (SCOTTISH) Bn. K.L.R.

Place	Date	Hour	Summary of Events and Information	Remarks and references to Appendices
ROBECQ, HAZEBROUCK, S.A. LENS II & CALAIS 13				9/11 37/16 47
VAUDRICOURT	1st May	Morning	Training Staff for training an American Batt. organised. Personnel as follows:- Majority, Batt. 2nd (Batty.) Adjutant Capt D.D. FARMER M.C. Company Comdrs. Capt W.A. DAVIDSON & Capt T.A. ROBERTS & (Capt A.R.S. HOUGHTON & 2nd Lt T.W. PILKINGTON from = 19th Bn) M.O. Capt T.H. STOWELL. Scout Officer 2nd Lt J. DARROCH M.C. Signal Officer Lieut T.E. COOKSON. Quarter Master 2nd Lieut G.W. MANSRIDGE Reviewing Officers:- Lieut T.H. STOWELL. Scout Officer 2nd Lt J. DARROCH M.C. Field W.O's N.C.O's & men = 54 (Instructors and Specialists)	16 7 sheets
"	"	"	Left by march route to join 55th Divn Depot Bn at 4.30 pm for ALLOUAGNE.	
ALLOUAGNE	2nd May		Resting & ordinary routine	
"	3rd "		Left by motor lorries to join 41st Ind Bde 16th (Irish) Divn at BLEQUIN billeted in village named NEUF MANOIR. 2nd Lt A. LAYTON 2nd London Regt joined the Trg Staff as Company Officer.	
NEUF-MANOIR	4th "		Ordinary Routine	
"	5th "		-"- -"-	
"	6th " 13 7th }		Ordinary Routine Training according orders to report to an American Batt.	
DESVRES	14th		Left NEUF MANOIR at 10.15 A.M. by march route for DESVRES	

WAR DIARY
or
INTELLIGENCE SUMMARY.

(Erase heading not required.)

TRAINING STAFF
2/10TH (SCOTTISH) Bn K.L.R.

Army Form C. 2118.

Place	Date	Hour	Summary of Events and Information	Remarks and references to Appendices
Rest Camp CALAIS	13	1000	Ordinary route training awaiting arrival of American Bn & making preparations for staff training	
DESVRES	15		" "	
"	16		" "	
"	17		Left DESVRES at 2.50 PM by march route for PARENTY	
PARENTY	18		Ordinary routine as above	
"	19 to 23		" "	
BEZINGHEM	24		Left PARENTY at 6 PM by march route for BEZINGHEM	
"	25 to 30		Ordinary training	
HESDIN L'ABBE	31		Left BEZINGHEM by march route at 6PM to join 148th Inf Brigade 16th (2nd) Divn. Bn Hq at CHAU. L'ENFER & Training Staff at HESDIN L'ABBE. Relieved Training Staff of 2nd Bn Musketry Regt. working with the infantry of the 37th Regt (American Inf.)	

O Lawton Lt
1/6/18
Cmdg "TRAINING STAFF" 2/10TH SCOTTISH Bn K.L.R.

WAR DIARY
INTELLIGENCE SUMMARY

Army Form C. 2118.

2/10th (Scottish) Bn K.L. Regt

Place	Date	Hour	Summary of Events and Information	Remarks and references to Appendices
CALAIS MAP 13. CHATEAU L'ENFER (5.C.61.85.)	JUNE 1st–8th		Ordinary Routine, assisting with the training of the 58th American Regiment.	
	9th		58th American Regiment departed	
	10th		320th American Regiment this 3rd Bn arrived	
	11th 12th		Ordinary Routine assisting with the training of the 320th American Regiment	
	18th		48th Inf Brigade (British) & 16th Division (British) England replaced by 101st Inf Bde & 34th Div & to which this Bn is now attached	17/7 2 sheets
	19th		Routine training	
	20th			
	21st		3rd Bn 320th American Regt arrived	
	22nd 26th 28th		Routine training	
	29th		101st Inf Bde & 34th Div (British) relieved by 117th Inf Bde & 39th Div (British) & this unit transferred to the latter	

WAR DIARY of 2/10 (Scottish) Bn K.L.R.

INTELLIGENCE SUMMARY.

Army Form C. 2118.

(Erase heading not required.)

Place	Date	Hour	Summary of Events and Information	Remarks and references to Appendices
MAP REF. CALAIS 13 1/100,000. CHATEAU L'ENFER	JUNE 30.		Ordinary Routine	
			Am Comme Cunnyn for O/C. Training Staff 2/10th (Scottish) Bn K.L.R.	

2/10TH (SCOTTISH) BN., KING'S LIVERPOOL REGT.

1918		Appendix.
June	CHATEAU L'ENFER.	
1st to 8th	Ordinary Routine, assisting with the training of the 58th American Regiment.	Ref. CALAIS MAP 13. (5C.61.85.) 1/100.000.
9th	58th American Regiment departed.	
10th	320th American Regiment less 3rd Bn arrived.	
11th to 17th	Ordinary Routine assisting with the training of the 320th American Regiment.	
18th	48th Inf Brigade (British) & 16th Division (British) left for England, replaced by 101st Inf. Bde, & 34th Div, to which this Bn is now attached.	
19th 20th	Routine training.	
21st	3rd Bn. 320th American Regt. arrived.	
22nd to 29th	Routine training. " "	
29th	101st Inf. Bde. & 34th Div. (British) relieved by 117th Inf. Bde. & 39th Div. (British) & this unit transferred to the latter.	
30th	Ordinary Routine.	

DON D. FARMER
Capt & Adjt.
for O.C.
TRAINING STAFF 2/10TH (SCOTTISH) BN.,
K.L.R.

19

WAR DIARY.

TO: D.A.G.

3rd Echelon.

I beg to enclose WAR DIARY for the
Month of JULY 1918, ~~please~~ also up to date of
"breaking up" of Unit viz 3rd August.

In the Field.   .... CAPTAIN,
21st August 1918.   O.C.
                        TRAINING STAFF 2/10th(Scottish)Bn.K.L.R.

2/10 Liverpools B 74
Army Form C. 2118/7
Training Staff
2/10 (Scottish) Bn K.L.R. Ceased

WAR DIARY
INTELLIGENCE SUMMARY
(Erase heading not required.)

Place	Date	Hour	Summary of Events and Information	Remarks and references to Appendices
CHATEAU HOURET	July 2 to 5th		Ordinary Training - interrupted by Training of with 308th Regiment American Army	
(Square 61.85)	6th		308th Regt departed from this area to neighbourhood of DOULLENS	
"	7th to 31st		Ordinary training of Training Staff. Awaiting arrival of American to do most of officers and N.C.O.s of courses	
"	Aug 1st		Orders received from 39th Divn to effect that this Unit would be "broken up". (Auth. 39th Divn 39/339/A.2 dated 31/7/18)	
"	" 2nd		Reformation completed for move.	
"	" 3rd		Re-Training Staff marched to & entrained from SAMER en route to ETAPLES	
ETAPLES	" "		Arrived ETAPLES. Orders received to join 1st Bn. with 300 ex 2nd Bn men on 12 Aug	
			In the field	Offg Comy Capt.
			— 31st Aug 1918	of Training Staff 2/10 (Scottish) Bn K.L.R.

57TH DIVISION
172ND INFY BDE

2-4TH STH LANCS REGT
1915 SEP — 1916 FEB
AND FEB 1917 – MAY 1919